10

Orthodox Christians in America

Religion in American Life

JON BUTLER & HARRY S. STOUT
GENERAL EDITORS

Orthodox Christians in America

John H. Erickson

OXFORD UNIVERSITY PRESS
New York • Oxford

For Paul and David

Oxford   New York
Athens Auckland Bangkok Bogotá Buenos Aires Calcutta
Cape Town Chennai Dar es Salaam Delhi Florence Hong Kong Istanbul
Karachi Kuala Lumpur Madrid Melbourne Mexico City Mumbai
Nairobi Paris São Paulo Singapore Taipei Tokyo Toronto Warsaw

and associated companies in
Berlin   Ibadan

Copyright © 1999 by John H. Erickson

Published by Oxford University Press, Inc.
198 Madison Avenue, New York, New York 10016
Website: www.oup-usa.org

Oxford is a registered trademark of Oxford University Press

Design: Loraine Machlin
Layout: Mary Neal Meador
Picture research: Lisa Kirchner

Library of Congress Cataloging-in-Publication Data

Erickson, John H.
    Orthodox Christians in America / John H. Erickson.
        p. cm. -- (Religion in American life)
    Includes bibliographical references and index.
    ISBN 0-19-510852-3 (alk. paper)
    I. Orthodox Eastern Church -- United States. I. Title.
    II. Series
    BX733.E75   1999   99-19901
281.9'73--DC21

9 8 7 6 5 4 3 2 1

Printed in the United States of America
on acid-free paper

On the cover: Holy Ascension Cathedral, Unalaska, by Xenia Oleksa.
    © Orthodox Church in America, 1996.
Frontispiece: Armenian archbishop Torkom Manoogian (center) releases 12 white doves
    into the air on Easter Sunday in St. Vartan Plaza in New York City.

Contents

Introduction

JON BUTLER & HARRY S. STOUT, GENERAL EDITORS

T he experience of Orthodox Christians remains one of the most fasci-
nating and mysterious stories of religion in American life. Orthodox
Christianity in America emanates from an astonishing variety of
sources—Russian missionaries in Alaska and Greek cotton merchants in New Orleans in the 19th century, Eastern Christians from
the Austro-Hungarian Empire, and immigrants from the Near East,
Ukraine, Romania, Bulgaria, and Albania throughout the 20th century. It
has made America a center of diverse expression honoring traditional
Eastern Christian belief and practice.

Orthodox Christians in America describes with clarity and vivid detail
the simultaneous importance of "right worship," ecclesiastical governance
and authority, and ethnic, national, and political differences among
Orthodox Christians in America. It traces Orthodoxy's efforts to uphold
traditional worship and church government in the New World, the search
for unity amidst so many differing national and ecclesiastical allegiances,
and the slow "Americanization" of the faith during its 200-year history in
the United States. Throughout all, it attests to the extraordinary vitality of
Orthodoxy in American history.

This book is part of a unique 17-volume series that explores the evo-
lution, character, and dynamics of religion in American life from 1500 to
the end of the 20th century. As late as the 1960s, historians paid relatively

little attention to religion beyond studies of New England's Puritans. But since then, American religious history and its contemporary expression have been the subject of intense inquiry. These new studies have thoroughly transformed our knowledge of almost every American religious group and have fully revised our understanding of religion's role in American history.

It is impossible to capture the flavor and character of the American experience without understanding the connections between secular activities and religion. Spirituality stood at the center of Native American societies before European colonization and has continued to do so long after. Religion—and the freedom to express it—motivated millions of immigrants to come to America from remarkably different cultures, and the exposure to new ideas and ways of living shaped their experience. It also fueled tension among different ethnic and racial groups in America and, regretfully, accounted for difficult episodes of bigotry in American society. Religion urged Americans to expand the nation—first within the continental United States, then through overseas conquests and missionary work—and has had a profound influence on American politics, from the era of the Puritans to the present. Finally, religion contributes to the extraordinary diversity that has, for four centuries, made the United States one of the world's most dynamic societies.

The Religion in American Life series explores the historical traditions that have made religious freedom and spiritual exploration central features of American society. It emphasizes the experience of religion in America—what men and women have understood by religion, how it has affected politics and society, and how Americans have used it to shape their daily lives.

Religion in American Life

JON BUTLER & HARRY S. STOUT
GENERAL EDITORS

Chapter 1

An Ancient Faith in the New World

A little Orthodox child once explained why he liked to go to church. "We usually get something," he said. And that certainly is true. Worshipers receive blessed fruit on the feast of Christ's transfiguration; holy water at Epiphany, the feast of his baptism; palms and pussy willows on Palm Sunday, to mark his entry into Jerusalem; an egg at Easter, the feast of his resurrection; sweet-smelling oil on the forehead at nearly every vigil service; something sweet to taste when receiving Holy Communion. No doubt this child's understanding of the Christian faith will become more sophisticated as he gets older. But even at a very early age, he has grasped something important. Without knowing the word "sacrament," he has understood its basic meaning: that God saves us in and through the stuff of this world—through the water of baptism, in which this child was immersed three times when still an infant; through the chrism, or perfumed oil, with which he was anointed afterward; through the consecrated bread and wine of the Eucharist, which the child receives each Sunday and feast day as communion in Christ's body and blood. Material things have been made holy through the incarnation of God's son, Jesus Christ. Creation has been restored to its proper relationship with God, making it a means of communion with God and with one's fellow human beings.

This sacramental approach to the world, which even our little child has begun to understand, is one of the most characteristic aspects of Orthodox Christianity. The handbooks of doctrine that this child one day may read speak of seven sacraments or "mysteries": baptism, chrismation (anointing of the newly baptized), Eucharist or Holy Communion, penance or confession of sins, ordination to the church's official ministry, marriage, and anointing of the sick. But the sacramental life of the church is not limited to these particularly solemn moments. It extends into the daily activities of ordinary Orthodox Christians through the icons, or images, of Christ and the saints that adorn their homes and churches; through the seasons of fasting and feasting, during which special foods are eaten, that mark the church year; and through gestures such as making the sign of the cross before meals and other important daily events.

The objects and gestures of Orthodoxy's sacramental life are part of the everyday experience of most Orthodox Christians—but what is familiar to them is not familiar to most Americans. Orthodoxy has been called the best-kept secret in America. Although there are many more than 4 million Orthodox Christians in the United States and Canada and more than 200 million worldwide, their history, beliefs, and practices remain generally unknown or misunderstood. In part this may be due to their uneven geographic distribution. Orthodox churches, often crowned by a dome or a cluster of cupolas, are part of the landscape in many northeastern cities and industrial towns, in Alaskan villages, and across the prairie provinces of Canada, but they are seldom seen in the towns and smaller cities of the western and southern states.

But even in regions where Orthodox Christians are relatively numerous, they remain an enigma. Often their faith and practices are known only from newspaper articles about the pageantry of Holy Week and Easter (which generally fall some weeks after western Christians have observed them) or the customs associated with Christmas (which for many Orthodox falls 13 days after the western observance). People who have read the novels of Russian writer Fyodor Dostoevsky may be familiar with certain aspects of Orthodox spirituality, and art-lovers may have encountered Orthodox icons. Yet even those who have a passing acquaintance with Orthodoxy may regard it as something foreign and long out of date, a picturesque remnant from an alien past.

Orthodoxy in America is perceived as exotic, and as fragmented. A glance through the yellow pages of the phone directory or through a reference work on religious denominations reveals a bewildering assortment of church names, some quite complex, that contain the word "Orthodox." Most of these names reflect the Old World roots of the groups in question in a straightforward manner: Greek Orthodox, Serbian Orthodox, Bulgarian Orthodox, Ukrainian Orthodox. But more than one group may employ the same ethnic designation. What difference is there, for example, between the Romanian Orthodox Archdiocese in America and Canada and the Romanian Orthodox Episcopate of America, or between the Russian Orthodox Church Outside Russia and the Russian Orthodox Church—Moscow Patriarchate? Names that appear self-evident sometimes may not be. In a medium-sized northeastern city, and possibly in the same neighborhood, you might find one parish calling itself Greek Orthodox, another calling itself Greek Catholic, another Russian Orthodox Greek Catholic, and another Carpatho-Russian Orthodox Greek Catholic. Beyond their overlapping names, what ties might unite these parishes? And what barriers might keep them apart?

In some cases, this bewildering array of names reflects divisions that can be traced back to the earliest centuries of Christianity. Other divisions have arisen more recently, some of them in the United States. In a few cases, the confusing variety of names reflects the fact that in America anyone can use words like Orthodox. A group can call itself the American

St. Theodosius Cathedral in Cleveland, Ohio, was dedicated in 1912. Its onion-shaped domes and cupolas recall those of churches in Russia.

Blessing of the waters forms part of the ritual for the feast of Epiphany. During the 1999 feast in Tarpon Springs, Florida, teenage boys race through the water to see who will retrieve the cross and be blessed with luck for the year. This ritual captures the sacramental sense of life important to every church member.

Holy Orthodox Catholic Apostolic Eastern Church without having any connection at all to historic Orthodox Christianity! Yet most of the groups that use the term Orthodox do so in the awareness that they share a common faith, a common way of life, and, to a high degree, a common history that distinguishes them from other Christians.

Some Orthodox Christians in the United States sport bumper stickers that read: "The Orthodox Church: Founded in 33 A.D." This is the year traditionally associated with Christ's crucifixion and resurrection. While this claim may sound pretentious, it does reflect the fact that the churches that today call themselves Orthodox have a strong sense of the historical ties linking them to the very beginnings of Christianity in ancient eastern Christian centers such as Jerusalem, Antioch, and Alexandria, where the church has had a more or less continuous history since New Testament times.

Christianity grew up in the Roman Empire, which at the time encompassed the entire Mediterranean world. The language that helped Christianity spread was Greek, the language of the New Testament. At that time Greek served as a universal language, in much the same way that English does today. Most of the major theologians, or religious teachers, of the early church wrote in Greek and lived in the eastern part of the empire, where Christianity was strongest. But Christianity was quickly embraced by people of many different cultures and languages— including Latin, Syriac, Coptic, and Armenian—both inside the empire and beyond its borders.

The church of these early Christians was not a single, unified structure. Most theologians and church historians today would describe it rather as a communion or family of local churches. These churches had their own local customs and distinctive ways of worshiping. They certainly did not insist on uniformity, but at the same time they were united in their sacramental life—above all in baptism and the Eucharist. Though scattered throughout the world, they regarded themselves as making up the same body of Christ, which they demonstrated whenever they received Holy Communion in the Eucharist. They also were united in the same apostolic faith, which meant that they claimed to hold the faith that was preached by the apostles, the men whom Christ had appointed to be witnesses to his saving work. But how could they maintain unity in faith, especially when this faith was threatened by heresy, or false teaching?

To overcome major challenges of this sort, the bishops who headed the local churches would meet together in councils. Some of these councils covered larger regions. They were organized and chaired by the primate, or chief bishop, of the region, who by the 5th century was called a

The Nicene Creed

For Orthodox Christians, this creed is the most fundamental statement of their beliefs. It was formulated at the first ecumenical, or universal, council of the church, held in the city of Nicæa in A.D. 325, and further developed at the second ecumenical council, held in Constantinople in A.D. 381.

I believe in one God, the Father almighty,
    maker of heaven and earth, and of all things visible and invisible;
And in one Lord, Jesus Christ, the Son of God,
    the only begotten, begotten of the Father before all ages,
    light of light, true God of true God,
    begotten, not made,
    of one essence with the Father;
    by whom all things were made;
    who for us men and for our salvation came down from heaven
    and was incarnate of the Holy Spirit and the Virgin Mary, and became man;
    and He was crucified for us under Pontius Pilate, and suffered and was buried;
    and the third day He rose again, according to the Scriptures,
    and ascended into heaven, and sits at the right hand of the Father;
    and He shall come again with glory to judge the living and the dead;
    whose kingdom shall have no end;
And in the Holy Spirit, the Lord, the giver of life, who proceeds from the Father;
    who with the Father and the Son together is worshiped and glorified;
    who spoke by the prophets;
In one holy, catholic, and apostolic Church;
I acknowledge one baptism for the remission of sins;
I await the resurrection of the dead and the life of the world to come.

metropolitan (because he headed the church of the metropolis, or capital city, of the region) or patriarch (the chief "father" of the people of a region). To this day, the Orthodox churches, stressing the need for common decision-making in each region, try to organize themselves in this way, with bishops regularly meeting together in councils under the presidency of their primate.

But in matters of particular urgency, when the integrity of the faith itself was challenged, an even wider gathering of bishops was needed: an ecumenical, or universal, council. The first of these ecumenical councils, the Council of Nicæa in A.D. 325, was especially important. Its creed, later expanded by the second ecumenical council in Constantinople in A.D. 381, became the touchstone for Orthodoxy throughout the Christian world. Even today, Orthodox Christians emphasize the authority of the Nicene Creed both in worship and teaching. Along with the Lord's Prayer, the creed is something that practically every Orthodox Christian child learns to say by heart.

Orthodox Christians, then, emphasize the importance of councils in the life of the church. Above all, they emphasize the authority of the early ecumenical councils, and they zealously insist on their own fidelity to the teachings of these councils. But sometimes rather than uniting these councils divided. In A.D. 451, the Council of Chalcedon met to address the question of how Jesus Christ could truly be one entity if he were both fully God and fully human. A major disagreement arose over the proper words for expressing this idea. The council spoke of Christ as "one person in two natures," divine and human, and most of the regional churches within the Roman Empire eventually accepted this wording. But some regional churches, particularly on the eastern borders of the empire, rejected it. While believing that Christ was both fully God and fully human, they preferred to speak of "one nature" in order to emphasize his unity. Their opponents labeled them "monophysites," from the Greek words *monos* and *physis,* meaning "one nature."

Apart from this important difference in theological terminology, the early churches were affected by political and cultural differences. Most of those who accepted the wording of the Council of Chalcedon were from the Greek- and Latin-speaking groups that dominated the life of the

Roman Empire at this time, while those who rejected it came from the Coptic (Egyptian), Syriac, and Armenian minorities, people who often felt separate from the empire and were out of its mainstream.

Despite attempts at reconciliation, the resulting division of the churches has lasted until the present day. Two distinct families of churches, both of which are represented in America, now call themselves Orthodox. The first group consists of the Chalcedonian or Eastern Orthodox churches. The other consists of the non-Chalcedonian or Oriental Orthodox churches. But although these two families of churches have been formally separated since the 5th century, they have continued to share the same sacramental approach to the world and the same emphasis on following the apostolic faith. Recent conversations between church leaders have led to the conclusion that the issues that initially divided the churches were about words, not substance, and leaders on both sides are now studying ways to restore full unity. Any developments along these lines could have important effects on the future of Orthodoxy in America. At the very least, the movement of these two families of churches toward unity suggests that fragmentation is not inevitable and that even long-standing historical divisions can be overcome.

The rise of Islam in the eastern Mediterranean in the seventh century swept away many of the structures for communication and cultural exchange that the Roman Empire had provided. Sea routes were disrupted. The old Roman roads decayed, making even land transportation difficult. The ancient centers of eastern Christianity in Syria, Palestine, and Egypt fell into decline. As travel and communication grew more difficult, the division between Chalcedonians and non-Chalcedonians hardened. But already a new center for eastern Christianity had emerged in Constantinople, the city that we now know as Istanbul, Turkey. Constantinople was founded by Emperor Constantine the Great in the 4th century to be the "New Rome" and co-capital of the empire. In the 9th century Constantinople entered its golden age as the "ruling city" of the vast Byzantine Empire, an empire that was still officially Roman but in culture was overwhelmingly Greek.

Missionaries went out from Constantinople, especially to the Slavic

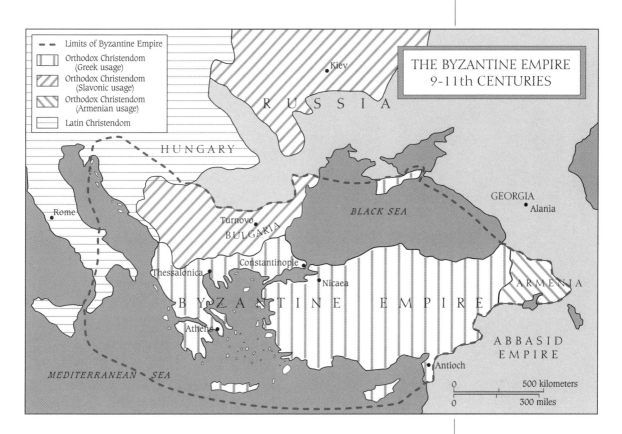

THE BYZANTINE EMPIRE
9-11th CENTURIES

Limits of Byzantine Empire

Orthodox Christendom (Greek usage)

Orthodox Christendom (Slavonic usage)

Orthodox Christendom (Armenian usage)

Latin Christendom

RUSSIA

Kiev

HUNGARY

Rome

Turnovo

BULGARIA

BLACK SEA

GEORGIA
• Alania

Thessalonica

Constantinople

• Nicaea

ARMENIA

BYZANTINE EMPIRE

Athens

ABBASID EMPIRE

MEDITERRANEAN SEA

• Antioch

0   500 kilometers

0   300 miles

peoples of the north. In the 9th century Sts. Cyril and Methodius set the pattern for missions in the Christian East. They emphasized the importance of adapting the ways of expressing the faith to the cultures of those who converted. For example, rather than making people learn Greek, they established a written Slavic language, now most often called Church Slavonic, and translated the texts needed for worship and other important works into it. Thus adapted, Eastern Orthodox Christianity became deeply embedded in the national cultures of the Bulgarian, Serbian, Ukrainian, and Russian peoples. The churches established in this way enjoyed a high degree of independence in managing their affairs, but they recognized Constantinople as their spiritual center.

Yet even as Constantinople was entering its golden age, its relations with Rome were growing strained. In the wake of the Germanic invasions that overwhelmed the western parts of the empire from the 5th cen-

Although ancient centers of Eastern Christianity in the Near East had fallen under Islamic rule by the 11th century, Byzantine cultural and religious influence was spreading among the Slavic peoples to the north of the empire.

The "Old Testament Trinity," by Andrei Rublev, is one of medieval Russia's most famous icons. To symbolize the Trinity, the icon depicts the three angels who, according to the account in the book of Genesis, appeared to Abraham.

tury onward, Rome had been left to its own devices. It had succeeded in converting the Germanic tribes to Latin Christianity without much use of native languages, and in the process it had helped to forge a relatively unified and uniform Latin Christian world in western Europe. By the 11th century this Latin Christian world was challenging the cultural and political dominance of Constantinople. Although in principle the churches of east and west remained one family, or communion, they had grown apart. In A.D. 1054 Rome and Constantinople broke communion with each other, formalizing the gap that had formed between them.

Contact between the eastern and western Christian churches did continue after 1054. It even intensified, as crusaders from the west swarmed eastward, intent on liberating the Holy Land from the forces of Islam. But in 1204, when the knights of the Fourth Crusade turned their attention instead to Constantinople, sacking it and forcibly imposing their own rule and church authorities, any real hope of reunion was lost. Separation gave way to the hostility that has characterized relations between the Orthodox church and the Roman Catholic church down to the 20th century. Since the events of 1204, Eastern Christians have been inclined to regard even the most well-meaning efforts toward reconciliation with suspicion.

Many of the issues on which the churches originally disagreed had to do with differences in liturgical practice and discipline. For example, the chief issue that gave rise to the schism of 1054 was whether leavened bread (as in the east) or unleavened bread (as in the west) should be used in the Eucharist. Even more divisive was the question of whether all orders of the clergy should be required to be celibate, or unmarried. In contrast to the Roman Catholic church, the Orthodox church has always permitted married men to be ordained as deacons and priests. (All bishops, however, are unmarried clergy who have taken vows as monks.)

Some serious theological issues also divided the churches. The most enduring of these has to do with the doctrine of the Trinity. Although Christians East and West believe in one God in three persons—Father, Son, and Holy Spirit—they have explained the relationship of these three persons in slightly different ways. In the early Middle Ages, the western church added the words "and from the Son" (*filioque*) to the Nicene Creed, so that it read, "I believe in the Holy Spirit . . . who proceeds from the Father *and from the Son*." Orthodox theologians believe that this phrase shows an incorrect understanding of the place of the Holy Spirit in the Trinity. They also have objected to the fact that the western church added the phrase without consulting the eastern church. They feel that this shows a lack of proper concern for the authority of the ancient ecumenical councils and that it ignores the early church's tradition of dealing with difficult issues through such councils.

Closely linked to disagreements over discipline and theology has been disagreement over authority in the church. The dispute centers on the question of papal primacy: What is the proper role of the bishop of Rome, or pope, in the church? During the Middle Ages, the pope's authority grew enormously in the west. Theologians and experts in church law even came to describe it in terms of monarchy. The Orthodox objected that such ideas could profoundly affect their faith. In their eyes, the Roman understanding of primacy went far beyond what the ancient ecumenical councils had envisioned. It appeared to undercut the eastern emphasis on conciliarity and group agreement by suggesting that the pope was more than just "first among equals" in relation to other bishops. Papal primacy also seemed to conflict with the eastern understanding of the church universal as a communion of local churches. The easterners felt that their churches' distinctive customs, discipline, and liturgical practices could be traced back to the apostles themselves. These features of their religion expressed the apostolic faith common to all the churches—they were not just "exceptions" to the Roman norm that had been approved by the pope.

The fall of Constantinople to the Ottoman Turks in 1453 reinforced the "easternness" of Orthodoxy and its differences from western forms of Christianity. Turkish rule throughout the Balkans and the Near East made Orthodox Christians into second-class citizens, heavily taxed and subject to an endless number of restrictions. But Islam did give other religious groups considerable freedom to manage their own affairs. The Orthodox Christians living in the Turkish Empire were regarded as a distinct people—the "Roman nation," or *rum milet,* as it was called in Turkish. The patriarch of Constantinople, assisted by the church hierarchy, was their leader not only in spiritual matters but in secular, or nonreligious, ones as well. On the one hand, this helped the Orthodox faithful remain unified in the face of Turkish oppression. On the other hand, it made the institutions that the patriarch supervised vulnerable to manipulation and corruption. Through the church hierarchy, wealthy Greek families with connections in the Ottoman court could wield enormous power over the entire "Roman nation," causing resentment among the Slavs, Arabs, and other non-Greek people. Long centuries of Turkish domination thus reinforced a sense of Orthodox identity in the subject peoples, but at the same time encouraged tensions among them.

While Ottoman rule was restricting Orthodox church life in the Balkans and the eastern Mediterranean, a new Orthodox power was rising to the north. That power was Russia, where the Orthodox faith flourished. Moscow emerged as a "third Rome." At the same time, however, the Russian Empire was open to many western influences. For example, Czar Peter the Great was very attracted by the political philosophy then current in Western Europe, which emphasized the absolute authority of the sovereign monarch in all aspects of life. This meant that secular authority was held to outrank religious authority. In line with this philosophy, Peter "reformed" the Russian church in 1721 by creating a state-dominated Holy Synod to head it instead of a patriarch. Despite this change, Russia took pride in its steadfast loyalty to the Orthodox faith, and it cheerfully took on the role of protector of Orthodox Christians within the Ottoman Empire and elsewhere. Not everyone appreciated this Russian involvement, however. Orthodox Slavs and Arabs generally welcomed Russian assistance, but the Greeks feared that the growing importance of the Russians would undermine their own leadership.

Orthodox unity was further undercut by the rise of nationalism in the 19th century. Wars of liberation in the Balkans resulted in the formation of new and sometimes competing nation-states: Greece, Serbia, Romania, Bulgaria, and Albania. These changes also produced new autocephalous, or "self-headed," Orthodox churches, beginning with the Church of Greece in 1850. While these churches were independent in the sense that they no longer fell under the jurisdiction of the patriarch of Constantinople, they generally were closely tied to the governments of the new nation-states. The church was considered an indispensable aspect of national life, but this meant that national politics often had a decisive impact on church life. By the beginning of the 20th century, Orthodoxy had become a sometimes quarrelsome family of self-governing autocephalous churches. The strength of these churches lay in their close identification with the needs and hopes of their people. Their weakness lay in the fact that they did not have effective ways to show their inner spiritual unity.

If you were to look at the Orthodox church only in terms of its history and institutions, it would indeed appear disorganized and fragmented. But most Orthodox Christians do not approach their church in that way. Their perception of the church is molded by their experience of its sacramental life, its life of worship, and only secondarily by its organizational politics or even by the letter of its doctrines. Worship is an essential aspect of Orthodoxy. The very word "orthodoxy" does not mean simply holding the right beliefs. It also means "right worship," the right way of giving glory—*doxa* in Greek—to God.

Many things illustrate the importance of worship for Orthodox Christians. Worship has played a major role in mission and evangelization, or spreading the faith. When Sts. Cyril and Methodius undertook their mission to the Slavs in the 9th century, they devised an alphabet that could be used to translate any text into the language of the local people—but almost all of the texts they translated were for use in worship services. A century later, when a delegation of still-pagan Slavs came to

The vast interior of Hagia Sophia, for centuries the center of Orthodox Christianity, was transformed into a mosque following the Turkish conquest of Constantinople in 1453.

Constantinople from Kiev on behalf of their prince, Vladimir, they were taken to services in the great church of Hagia Sophia, the church of the Holy Wisdom. Earlier, these Slavs had found the worship of the Muslims "abominable" and that of the Germans "lacking in beauty." Worship in Hagia Sophia was very different: "We knew not whether we were in heaven or on earth, for on earth there is no such splendor or beauty, and we are at a loss how to describe it. We only know that God dwells there." Over the centuries, the compelling beauty of Orthodox worship has brought millions to Christianity—not only Slavs and other Eastern Europeans but also Africans, Indians, Japanese, Native Americans, and countless other groups. It has shaped their understanding of the Christian faith and helped them maintain their Christian identity not only when great temples like Hagia Sophia were functioning as churches but also in times when Christians were persecuted or kept on the outskirts of society.

If you go beyond the confusing picture of Orthodoxy presented in the Yellow Pages, church directories, and other reference works, if you locate an Orthodox church of whatever tradition, Eastern or Oriental, and step inside to witness a service, you will probably be struck by how different the atmosphere is from what you might expect to find in a house of worship. The many icons, the rich vestments of the clergy, the clouds of incense, the postures and gestures of the worshipers, the melodies of the seemingly endless chants—all this can be overwhelming, bewildering, and perhaps even troubling. People who are used to a less formal style of worship or to church services that involve a great deal of instruction may question the point of so much ritual. But the point of this elaborate ritual really is very simple: to communicate the basic truths of the Christian faith through "right worship," in ways that go beyond mere words.

"Right worship" conveys a sense of the majesty of the almighty God. Through the slow but steady pace of the long service, with its many litanies, majestic hymns, and lofty prayers, worshipers are invited to enter into the rhythm and beauty of a heavenly liturgy, to join with the angels in their never-ending songs of praise. As a hymn sung at the Divine Liturgy (as the Orthodox call their eucharistic service) says,

> Let us who mystically represent the cherubim
> and sing the thrice-holy hymn to the life-creating Trinity
> now lay aside all earthly cares,
> so that we may receive the king of all,
> who comes invisibly upborne by the angelic hosts.
> Alleluia, alleluia, alleluia!

At the same time, "right worship" conveys a sense of God's concern "for us and for our salvation," as the Nicene Creed puts it. God has revealed his love for us through the mystery of the incarnation of his Son. The liturgical prayers and hymns of the Orthodox church sum up the meaning of this mystery in words of rich theological content. But Orthodox worship does not rely simply on words, as though Christianity were meant only for intellectuals with a taste for religious discussion. Orthodox worship is very tangible. It appeals to all the senses. In this way, it tries to make the meaning of the incarnation readily accessible to everyone. The little child thrilled to "get something" whenever he goes to church can get a sense of this mystery as easily as a well-educated and theologically literate adult.

"Right worship" gives Orthodox Christians a knowledge of the Christian faith based in their own experience. It also gives them their sense of

Members of the Federated Russian Orthodox Clubs sing in St. Mary's Cathedral in Minneapolis, Minnesota. Singing takes place throughout services in the Orthodox Church, making the role of the choir or the cantor extremely important.

solidarity as a community. Visitors to an Orthodox church often are struck by the way that everyone seems to feel at home. Everyone seems to know his or her proper place and task. A middle-aged gentleman, perhaps the president of the parish council, supervises the sale of candles. A woman rushes in, possibly a little late, with an armful of flowers that she arranges around the icons. A young mother exits without embarrassment to quiet her crying child. An old lady stands silently in prayer. The clergy and altar servers play a prominent role, but so do the cantors or choir, because there is singing throughout Orthodox services. In all this, everyone seems to have a good idea of what will happen next. One of the happier consequences of having a stable liturgy with predictable words and actions is that everyone knows its basic rules. The clergy are not "experts" in the sense that they are apart from and directing the actions of everyone else. Each one of the faithful, from the little

child to the old lady, in some sense is performing a ministry. Each is a valued member of the same body of Christ.

The sense of community created in Orthodox worship is not limited to those who are physically present. The icons of the saints, their commemoration in the course of the church year, and the names of the dead mentioned during church services all contribute to a powerful sense of tradition. Orthodox worshipers share a sense of the continuity of their church through the centuries despite the rise and fall of empires. It is the act of worship, more than councils or creeds, that has given Orthodox Christians their identity, their sense of being "at home" in the church and of belonging to it. Of course, Orthodox worship, like other aspects of the church's life, has undergone historical development. It is not static, utterly unchanged and unchanging. But on the whole the Orthodox liturgical tradition, whether in the Chalcedonian or the non-Chalcedonian version, has been very conservative. It has not experienced the kinds of disruptions and revolutions that western Christian worship experienced—at the time of the Protestant Reformation in the 16th century, for example. The conservative nature of the Orthodox liturgy has helped make worship the standard for practically all aspects of church life, to a degree unmatched in the western Christian churches.

Orthodox respect for tradition expresses itself in many ways. In general, Orthodox Christians are very suspicious of novelty and innovation in religious matters, whether in doctrine or in worship. It is significant that in the course of disputes with the Roman Catholic church, easterners denounced the western addition of the word *filioque* to the creed precisely because it was an innovation. Orthodox Christians believe that respect for tradition has enabled their church to preserve the authentic apostolic faith from the earliest days of Christianity, with nothing added to it or taken from it. But, as many modern Orthodox theologians have observed, respect for tradition can easily degenerate into a stiff and formal traditionalism, in which people maintain outward forms without concern for the inner content of worship. Resistance to change of any sort is not necessarily a good thing. As these theologians have pointed out, since its earliest times the Orthodox church has had to address new situations and make its presence felt in new contexts. Its true tradition has always been a *living* tradition.

Ordinary Orthodox Christians do not always find it easy to distinguish an appropriate adaptation to new circumstances from a betrayal of "right worship." In the past, major schisms, or splits between groups of the faithful, have resulted from seemingly minor changes. In 17th-century Russia, the "Old Believers' schism" arose because of changes in such things as the pronunciation of the word "alleluia," the proper way of making the sign of the cross, and the direction of processions around the church building on holy days.

In the 20th century, similar issues have caused controversy both in the Old World and in America. The calendar is one example. Until the 20th century, all Orthodox churches used the Julian calendar, introduced in the Mediterranean world by Julius Caesar in the first century B.C. Orthodox Christians criticized the new Gregorian calendar, introduced in Europe in the 16th century by Pope Gregory XIII, as an innovation. But since 1923, many Orthodox churches have adopted the "new calendar" for fixed-date feasts such as Christmas, while keeping the old way of calculating the date of Easter. The change from "old" to "new" has not always gone smoothly. At times, conflict between "New Calendarists" and "Old Calendarists" has threatened not only relations between the autocephalous Orthodox churches but also the unity and harmony of local church communities.

Today, the Eastern Orthodox church includes 13 universally recognized autocephalous churches, as well as two whose autocephalous status is disputed. There are also two autonomous churches, which can manage their own affairs and choose their own bishops but must be headed by someone who is confirmed by another church. The heads of the most ancient and largest of the Eastern Orthodox churches are called patriarchs. The heads of the newer and smaller churches usually have the title of metropolitan or archbishop. The various Orthodox churches or "jurisdictions" in America are linked to their autocephalous "mother churches" in the Old World in various ways.

The non-Chalcedonian or Oriental Orthodox family of churches today consists of six churches. Like the Eastern Orthodox churches, most of these Oriental Orthodox churches have faithful in America as well as in the Old World, and in most cases they too have organized their own jurisdictions in America to minister to their spiritual needs.

In a rapidly changing world, all of these churches, both Eastern and Oriental, face new challenges. Especially since the fall of communism in Eastern Europe, many have new opportunities for internal renewal and external cooperation. All have greater possibilities than ever before for showing unity and overcoming the isolation and fragmentation that has tended to characterize them in the past. At the same time, they must contend with a new burst of nationalism and other powerful forces that could easily drive them further apart. How the Old World churches meet these challenges will have enormous consequences for Orthodox Christians in America, who have always had close ties with their "mother churches." But the future of Orthodoxy in America does not depend simply on the Orthodox churches of the Old World. If Orthodoxy is to be more than an exotic museum-piece, Orthodox Christians in America must rediscover its living tradition.

ПРᴨД. ГЕ́РМАНЪ
АЛѦСКИНСКІЙ

SAINT HERMAN
OF ALASKA

Chapter 2

Entrepreneurs and Missionaries

As Columbus discovered, it is possible to reach America from Europe by sailing west across the Atlantic. That was the route taken by the successive waves of immigrants from whose perspective American history—and the history of religion in America—has often been written. But it is also possible to reach America by traveling east across Siberia to the Pacific rim and from there across the Bering Straits to Alaska, following the route taken thousands of years before by the earliest immigrants, the ancestors of the Native Americans. Orthodox Christians reached America by both routes. Their unusually complex history does not conform neatly to familiar patterns. It is a story of immigration but also one of mission. The Orthodox Christians not only struggled to preserve their ancient faith in the New World, but also labored to share that faith with others.

The earliest history of Orthodoxy in North America is bound up with efforts by the European powers to develop colonial empires in the New World. In 1763, after decades of intermittent war, Florida passed from Spanish to British rule. Generous land grants from the British crown encouraged entrepreneurs to establish colonies in the new territories. Among these colonizers was Andrew Turnbull, a Scottish physician married to the daughter of a wealthy Greek merchant. In 1766 Turnbull secured a grant of 20,000 acres, which he named New Smyrna in honor

Vitus Bering, a Danish navigator in the service of Russia, was the first European explorer to sight and map the Alaskan coast. The chain and anchor of his memorial are said to have come from his ship, which was wrecked on the return voyage to Russia.

of his wife's birthplace, the city of Smyrna in what is now Turkey. Financed by the London Board of Trade, he sailed to the Mediterranean to recruit colonists. Turnbull directed his attention especially toward Greeks, reasoning that they would be eager for freedom from Turkish oppression and would adapt easily to the Florida climate. He even gave some thought to providing an Orthodox priest to serve the colony's spiritual needs. But like many of Turnbull's ambitious plans, this one never materialized. The recruits arrived priestless at their destination in the summer of 1768. Within two years more than half of them were dead of disease, malnourishment, and brutal working conditions. Those who survived fled to St. Augustine, 75 miles to the north, and by 1777 New Smyrna was abandoned. The first mass settlement of Orthodox Christians in America had disappeared, leaving scarcely a trace.

As Great Britain struggled with Spain for control of Florida, another major European power, Russia, was tightening its hold on the opposite extremity of the North American continent, in Alaska. During the 16th and 17th centuries, Russian explorers and traders had pressed east across Siberia to the shores of the Pacific Ocean. Before his death in 1725, Czar Peter the Great had laid plans for the systematic exploration of lands still farther east. Vitus Bering, a Dane working for Russia, led an expedition into the North Pacific in 1728 but failed to sight North America. He and Alexis Chirikov led a second eastern expedition in 1741. After mapping some of the Aleutian Islands, they sighted the Alaskan mainland. On July 20, 1741, aboard the ship *St. Peter,* Father Hilarion Trusov celebrated the first Orthodox Divine Liturgy, or Eucharist, in America. The return voyage was marred by shipwreck, disease, and the death of many of the company, including Bering, but the expedition had achieved its scientific goal of charting the northwestern coast of North America. It also carried home a valuable cargo of sea otter pelts, touching off a "fur rush" to Alaska.

For the next half century independent Russian trapper-traders, called *promyshlenniki,* plied the Alaskan waters in search of quick wealth. Their greed provoked occasional resistance from the native peoples, but in time many of the Russians settled permanently in America, learning native languages, marrying native women, and adopting native ways. So completely did they assimilate that by the end of the century, when British explorer Captain James Cook visited the Aleutian Islands, he found it impossible to tell the Russians from native Alaskans. But although they had adopted a native Alaskan way of life, the *promyshlenniki* maintained their Orthodox beliefs and practices even without ordained clergy. They baptized their native wives and children and taught them the basics of the Christian faith. When the first priest to reside on Unalaska Island arrived in 1795, he found the inhabitants already baptized.

But the days of the independent *promyshlenniki* were numbered. By the 1780s a wealthy Siberian merchant named Gregory Shelikov was arguing for the establishment of permanent trading posts in Alaska. These, he argued, would permit more efficient exploitation of Alaska's natural resources and extend Russian military and political influence around the Pacific rim. With his business partner Ivan Golikov, Shelikov established a small Russian colony on Kodiak Island in 1784. Three years later he traveled to the imperial court in St. Petersburg to boast of his accomplishments and to seek sole control of the fur trade. Empress Catherine the Great was not greatly impressed. Shelikov's company did not gain its coveted monopoly until 1799, when her successor, Emperor

Bering led two major expeditions to North America. His discoveries laid the groundwork for more than a century of Russian rule in Alaska.

Gregory Shelikov, Siberian fur trader and merchant, established the first permanent Russian trading outpost in Alaska, on Kodiak Island, in 1784.

Paul I, chartered it as the Russian-American Company.

But at least one prominent figure was moved by Shelikov's pleas. With characteristic exaggeration, Shelikov had written to Metropolitan Gabriel of St. Petersburg, one of the highest-ranking churchmen in the Russian Empire, boasting of the number of natives whom he had baptized and of the many native children who were attending the company school and company chapel—neither of which existed! Shelikov begged that a priest be assigned to his fledgling colony and promised that the company would cover all expenses. Metropolitan Gabriel responded by recruiting an entire missionary team from the Valaam Monastery, a famous center of spirituality and mission located on Russia's border with Finland. On December 25, 1793, a band of eight monks, headed by Archimandrite (Abbot) Joasaph, left St. Petersburg for America. After a journey of 293 days and 7,327 miles, they arrived on Kodiak on September 24, 1794. They had traveled a third of the way around the world without leaving the Russian Empire.

Archimandrite Joasaph and his associates knew very well that they were the heirs of a long tradition of monastic mission in the Christian East. They could look back at Sts. Cyril and Methodius, the 9th-century evangelizers of the Slavs; at the monks who had provided the Ukrainians and Russians with living examples of Christian virtue following the conversion of Prince Vladimir in A.D. 988; and at St. Stephen of Perm, whose labors among the Zyrian people in Siberia included the invention of a Zyrian alphabet and translation of the gospel. Once on Kodiak the missionaries energetically began imitating these great models. Writing to his spiritual father at the Valaam Monastery nine months later, Abbot Joasaph stated: "I have, praise God, baptized more than 7,000 Americans, and celebrated more than 2,000 weddings. We have built a church and, if time allows, we shall build another, and two portable ones, but a fifth is needed. We live comfortably, they love us and we them. They are a kind people, but poor. They take baptism so much to heart that they smash and burn all the magic charms given them by the shamans."

The missionaries faced many unexpected hardships, however. When they arrived in Alaska, they discovered that the church and supplies promised by Shelikov did not exist. But their greatest trials came at the hands of the all-powerful company manager, Alexander Baranov. They were appalled by the brutality with which Baranov and his men treated the Native Americans. The Russians forced hunters to work at gunpoint, kept young women as their mistresses, and separated small children from their mothers. The Eastern monastic tradition insisted on the right and duty of monks to seek help from the authorities on behalf of the oppressed, and, true to this tradition, Joasaph sent vivid reports of abuse back to Shelikov: "Since my arrival at this harbor I have seen nothing done to carry out your good intentions. My own pleasure is that so many Americans are coming from everywhere to be baptized, but the Russians not only make no effort to encourage them, but use every means to discourage them. The reason for this is that their depraved lives become evident if compared to the good conduct of the Americans." Receiving no reply from Shelikov, Joasaph and two other monks returned to Russia in 1798 to report firsthand on conditions in the colony and to raise support for the creation of a seminary in Alaska to train native clergy. In Russia Joasaph was ordained bishop of Kodiak, a position that would give him moral and political influence far greater than Baranov's, and he received books and other supplies for his projected seminary. On the voyage back to Alaska in 1799, however, his ship sank in heavy seas. All on board perished.

Even before the death of Joasaph and his companions, the mission had lost one of its most energetic members, Father Juvenaly, who was killed by hostile natives while on a preaching expedition into the Alaskan interior in 1796. Now the disaster at sea reduced it still more. Nevertheless, with the monk Herman in charge, the missionaries continued to defend the native Alaskans. In 1800 Baranov retaliated by placing them under house arrest and forbidding further contact with the natives. Within a year the missionaries infuriated Baranov still more by attempting to have the natives take the oath of allegiance to the czar, which would have given them the legal protection of Russian citizens. This time Baranov threatened to put the missionaries in irons.

Some hope for improvement came when the Holy Synod, the highest administrative body of the Russian church, appointed a high-ranking monk named Gideon to inspect the colony and revive the flagging mission. During his three-year visit, Gideon gained a shrewd appreciation of the source of the mission's problems. He reported to his superiors in Russia that "the personal insults which the missionaries endured from the employees of the company were the results of the prevailing attitude that 'God is in heaven, the czar is far away,' and only Baranov is to be feared." Unfortunately, Gideon's report was undercut by letters from Nicholas Rezanov, a company representative, who defended Baranov and belittled the monks as "incapable of comprehending the broad purposes of the government and of the company."

Continuing complaints against the management of the Russian-American Company led to yet another official

The double-headed eagle crest was a symbol of imperial authority that Russia adopted from the Byzantine Empire. It was used in America and elsewhere to mark Russian territorial claims.

inquiry, this one conducted by Captain Vasily Golovnin in 1818. He was favorably impressed by the simple piety and good sense of Father Herman and took seriously his frank assessment of Baranov's regime. The government took Golovnin's findings into account when the Russian-American Company's charter came up for renewal in 1821. The new charter subjected the company to much closer government supervision and strengthened the position of the clergy. But already condi-tions in Alaska were changing. Baranov had retired to Russia a few months before Golovnin's arrival. His replacement, Simeon Yanovsky, admitted that at first he had believed slanderous stories that claimed Father Herman was encouraging the natives to rise in rebellion against the authori-ties, but after meeting Father Herman and viewing the situation personally, he had changed his opinion. This well-read and cosmopolitan gentleman later would write to the abbot of the Valaam Monastery: "To my great surprise, the simple, uneducated monk Father Herman, inspired by God's grace, spoke so skillfully, forcefully and convincingly, and offered such proof, that no learning or earthly wisdom could stand against it!" In time Yanovsky came to regard Father Herman as his spiritual mentor, and after the death of his wife, he himself became a monk.

Father Herman, the last surviving member of the original mission team, spent his last years in seclusion on Spruce Island, not far from Kodiak. He named his little hermitage "New Valaam," after his old monastery in Russia. There he followed a strict monastic way of life that was both physically and spiritually rigorous. He slept on a wooden bench with a brick for his pillow, wore the simplest of homemade clothes, and spent much of his time in prayer. But he also ran a school, nursed the sick, cared for numerous orphans, and raised food for himself and the orphans in his experimental garden. Before his death Father Herman revealed to the natives of Spruce Island what was ahead for them and him. He told them that no priest would be available to bury him and that they would have to do this themselves. He also predicted that he would be forgotten for 30 years but then be remembered. When he died on December 13, 1837, he was buried in the way he had foretold, practically forgotten by the outside world. Although the natives of Spruce Island continued to revere the memory of their saintly "grandfather," *Apa* Herman, it was only in 1867—30 years later—that the Russian Orthodox church began to investigate his life. Belief in Father Herman's holiness spread, and in 1970 he was canonized as the first Orthodox saint of America.

Under its new 1821 charter, the Russian-American Company had to provide and support enough priests and other church workers to serve the religious needs of its far-flung North American holdings. But these provisions might have remained a dead letter had it not been for a new zeal for missions within the Russian Orthodox church. Governmental reforms were stressing the multinational character of the Russian Empire, and the church responded by sending missionaries to the many tribes of its eastern territories, devising alphabets for the native languages, translating scriptures and service books, and training native clergy. The North American colonies were among the beneficiaries of this program.

Most famous among this new wave of missionaries was Father John Veniaminov, who in 1824 arrived on the island of Unalaska with his wife and family. He quickly learned the local dialect of the Aleut language, developed an alphabet, and compiled a dictionary. With the help of a local native chief, Ivan Pan'kov, he translated the Gospel of St. Matthew and parts of the Divine Liturgy and even wrote a small catechism in Aleut, entitled *Indication of the Pathway into the Kingdom of Heaven.* A jack-of-all-trades, Veniaminov taught the natives the basics of carpentry and metalwork, and together they built Unalaska's Church of the Ascension. He and his wife Catherine also established an orphanage and a school, where more than 100 boys and girls learned trades as well as reading (both Aleut and Russian), writing, and arithmetic. From Unalaska Veniaminov traveled by kayak throughout the Aleutian Islands to teach and baptize. He was an effective communicator. Years later an aged Aleut would recall that "when he preached the Word of God, all the people listened without moving until he stopped. Nobody thought of fishing or hunting while he spoke; nobody felt hungry or thirsty as long as he was speaking, not even little children." Everywhere he went, Veniaminov took careful notes on local geology, climate, population, customs, plants, and wildlife. His three-volume *Notes on the Islands of the Unalaska District* and other scientific works eventually earned him membership in Russia's prestigious Imperial Academy of Sciences.

In 1834 the governor of Alaska, Baron Ferdinand von Wrangell, persuaded Veniaminov to move to Sitka, then called New Archangel, the capital of Russian America. There Veniaminov set about learning the

Father John (later Bishop Innocent) Veniaminov made this mantle clock. Other examples of his craftsmanship include chairs, cabinets, and an ingenious perpetual calendar that made use of movable pegs to mark the passage of the days, weeks, and months of the church year.

Bishop Innocent Veniaminov's
Instructions for Missionaries

During the decades of his missionary work in Alaska, Bishop Innocent Veniaminov always valued the dignity of the native people whom he served, respected their culture, and refused to rely on the superior material resources offered by the Russian presence in Alaska. In 1853 he issued "Instructions to the Priest-Monk Theophan" for the guidance of a missionary in the Nushagak region of Alaska. This section summarizes Bishop Innocent's approach to mission.

- On arriving at some settlement of savages, thou shalt on no account say that thou art sent by any government, or give thyself out for some kind of official functionary, but appear in the guise of a poor wanderer, a sincere well-wisher to his fellow-men, who has come for the single purpose of showing them the means to attain prosperity and, as far as possible, guiding them in their quest.

- From the moment when thou first enterest on thy duties, do thou strive, by conduct and by virtues becoming thy dignity, to win the good opinion and respect not alone of the natives, but of the civilized residents as well. Good opinion breeds respect, and one who is not respected will not be listened to.

- On no account show open contempt for their manner of living, customs, etc., however these may appear deserving of it, for nothing insults and irritates savages so much as showing them open contempt and making fun of them and anything belonging to them.

- From thy first interview with natives, do thy best to win their confidence and friendly regard, not by gifts or flattery, but by wise kindliness, by constant readiness to help in every way, by good and sensible advice and sincerity. For who will open his heart to thee, unless he trust thee?

- In giving instruction and talking with natives generally, be gentle, pleasant, simple, and in no way assume an overbearing, didactic manner, for by so doing thou canst seriously jeopardize the success of thy labors.

- When a native speaks to thee, hear him out attentively, courteously and patiently, and answer questions convincingly, carefully and kindly; for any question asked by a native on spiritual subjects is a matter of great

St. Innocent Veniaminov (1797-1879) was the first Orthodox bishop in America. His approach to mission helped to ensure that an indigenous Orthodox Church would survive in Alaska even after the end of Russian rule.

importance to the preacher, since it may be an indication both of the state of the questioner's soul and of his capacity, as well as of his desire, to learn. But by not answering him even only once, or answering in a way at which he can take offense, he may be silenced forever.

- Those who show no wish to receive holy baptism, even after repeated persuasion, should not in any way be vexed, nor, especially, coerced. And although justice demands that converts and such as are ready to become converts should be treated with greater kindness and consideration, still thou, as preacher of the Gospel, shouldst not be insulting in thy treatment of such as show no disposition to listen to instruction, but shouldst be friendly in thy intercourse with them. This will be to them the best proof that thou dost really and truly wish them well.

language and culture of the local Tlingit Indians, who traditionally had been hostile toward the Russians and their Aleutian confederates. Veniaminov made few conversions at first, but managed to gain the Tlingits' confidence when he helped combat a smallpox epidemic by undertaking a program of immunization. During his years in Sitka Veniaminov did not have to travel as frequently as when at Unalaska, but his parish did include the most distant outpost of the Russian-American Company: Fort Ross, about 80 miles north of San Francisco. Established in 1812, this old trading post was nearing the end of its years under Russian rule, but it still served as the base of operations for a mixed flock of about 260 men and women. In 1836 Veniaminov made a six-week pastoral visit to Fort Ross. On his return trip he toured the Spanish missions of San Rafael, San Jose, Santa Clara, and San Francisco. He conversed with the Spanish fathers in Latin, which he had learned in the seminary, and as a token of appreciation for their hospitality, he built several small barrel-organs for them upon his return to Sitka.

In 1839 Veniaminov traveled to European Russia to arrange for the publication of his scientific studies, report on his mission work, and press for the establishment of a separate diocese for Alaska, which hitherto had been part of the diocese of Irkutsk, in Siberia. (A diocese is a church district under the supervision of a bishop.) While there, he learned of the death of his wife. After being assured that his children would be cared for by the church, Veniaminov took monastic vows, taking the name of Innocent, and in December 1840 he was ordained as bishop of the newly established diocese of Kamchatka (in eastern Siberia) and the Kurile and Aleutian Islands. Bishop Innocent (Orthodox bishops are generally addressed and referred to by their first names) returned to Sitka the following year. For the next 18 years he supervised a remarkable expansion of the mission into the interior and northern coastal regions of Alaska. In Sitka he launched a major building campaign that produced the Mission House and its Annunciation Chapel (the oldest structure still standing in Alaska), and St. Michael's Cathedral, consecrated in 1848 in the presence of nearly 50 clergy of the Alaska mission. This dramatic rise in the

Church members raise the cross on the bell tower of St. Michael's Cathedral in Sitka, Alaska. St. Innocent Veniaminov, who was bishop when the cathedral was consecrated in 1848, built the large clock in the tower with his own hands.

number of clergy was due above all to another of Bishop Innocent's projects, a seminary where native and creole, or mixed-race, candidates for ordination studied not only theology but also native languages (Aleutian, Eskimo, and Tlingit), medicine, and Latin.

Bishop Innocent was raised to the rank of archbishop in 1850, with an expanded jurisdiction that covered much of eastern Siberia. An auxiliary, or assistant, bishop was appointed to serve the now well-established Alaskan church, and Innocent went to Siberia, where he learned yet another native language and continued his missionary work. In 1868 he was named metropolitan of Moscow, making him the highest-ranking churchman in the Russian Empire. Though nearly blind and in constant pain from legs crippled by years of travel by kayak, Metropolitan Innocent continued to emphasize the importance of mission. In 1870 he

An amension is a cloth into which relics are sewn. It is placed on top of an unconsecrated altar so that the Eucharist can be celebrated there. St. Innocent signed this amension when he was the bishop of Kamchatka in the Kuril and Aleutian Islands.

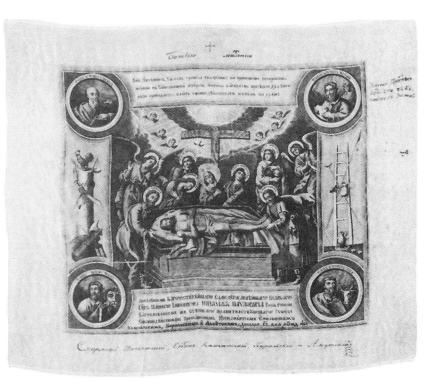

founded the Orthodox Missionary Society, which would help to finance the work of the Alaskan mission until the Communist revolution of 1917. The great missionary died on March 31, 1879, at the age of 82. In 1977 he was canonized by the Russian Orthodox church as "Saint Innocent, Enlightener of the Aleuts and Apostle to America."

Among Veniaminov's associates in America, none accomplished more than Jacob Netsvetov, a Creole of Aleut and Russian ancestry. After completing seminary studies in Siberia, Netsvetov was ordained in 1828 to assist Veniaminov in the evangelization of the Aleutian Islands. Despite the death of his wife and many other personal calamities, with Veniaminov's encouragement Netsvetov devoted himself to translation, native education, and other missionary activities. Once a bishop, Veniaminov assigned Netsvetov to begin missionary work in the Yukon River delta region among the Yup'ik Eskimo. This marked a new stage in the Alaskan mission. For 18 years Netsvetov and his native and creole associates carried on their labors hundreds of miles from the nearest Russian settlement, without protection or physical support from the civil authorities. It was no easy task. Not only were the physical conditions challenging, but the native peoples of the region did not always get along with one another. At one point Netsvetov was invited to preach to the Athabascan Indian tribes. He succeeded in converting and baptizing hundreds of people, in the process narrowly averting a tribal war. In his diary he recorded the event: "What a joy to see so many joined to the Church of Christ, former enemies now living together in peaceful coexistence!"

By the time of Netsvetov's death in 1865, a vibrant Alaskan Orthodox culture had developed. Native and creole people were taking a dominant role in the economic and religious life of this distant outpost of the Russian Empire. According to the 1860 government census, Sitka had a population of 1024, of whom 452 were Russians. In the Kodiak district, only 67

Sitka was the capital of Alaska between 1802 and 1900. St. Michael's Cathedral and the 1845 Mission House, built when Sitka was still called New Archangel and was the capital of Russian America, remain prominent landmarks.

45

out of a total population of 3,086 were Russian, and in other districts the Russian population was even less significant—in all the Aleutian Islands, for example, there were only eight Russians. But the church numbered approximately 12,000 Alaskan Christians in 43 communities, with 9 permanent churches, 35 chapels, 17 schools, and 4 orphanages. It was largely through the work of native leaders, including dozens of lay readers and church wardens as well as clergy, that the church in Alaska was able to survive—and even at times to thrive—after Russia sold Alaska to the United States in 1867.

For some in the Russian Orthodox church, the sale of Alaska to the United States represented a new opportunity. Back in Russia, Metropolitan Innocent Veniaminov saw it as "one of the ways of Providence by which our Orthodoxy can insert itself into the United States." In a letter to the imperial Russian minister for Orthodox church affairs, he sketched a number of measures to encourage the mission of the Orthodox church throughout North America: The headquarters of the bishop should be transferred from Sitka to San Francisco; an English-speaking bishop and staff should be appointed; the clergy should be allowed to use English in church services; service books and other materials should be translated into English; and pastoral schools should be established to train future clergy, in which "the curriculum must be in English and not in Russian, which will sooner or later be replaced by the former language."

The sale of Alaska did offer new opportunities for the Orthodox mission in the New World, but it also presented some unprecedented problems and challenges. While the 1867 treaty that made Alaska part of the United States promised that the Orthodox church could retain its property in Alaska and continue its mission, protected by American constitutional guarantees of freedom of religion, it did little to protect the property or cultural heritage of the native population. The government of the United States, engaged in successive Indian wars as white settlers pushed westward, had little appreciation for Alaska's natives and Creoles. Although these people suffered minimal physical violence, U.S. soldiers stationed in Sitka rioted and looted St. Michael's Cathedral and a naval gunboat shelled several Tlingit villages. For the most part, the battle for the Alaskan native peoples was fought out in the classroom, through aggressive programs intended to replace native culture, which now included the Orthodox faith as an important element, with Anglo-American culture and mainstream Protestant values.

An important leader in this campaign of Americanization and assimilation was Sheldon Jackson, a Presbyterian minister whose social and political connections in Washington gained him appointment as Alaska's first commissioner of education (1885–1906). Following what was then standard on American Indian reservations, Jackson encouraged the establishment of boarding schools run by federally funded Protestant missions. Native and creole children would be removed from their homes, sometimes by force, and enrolled in these schools in order to bring them to "the Anglo-Saxon frame of mind."

In contrast to the Orthodox mission's two- or three-language approach to education, these boarding schools insisted that students use only English, even when speaking among themselves. One of Jackson's associates, the Reverend S. Hall Young, explained this policy in his autobiography: "One strong stand, so far as I know I was the first to take, was the determination to do no translating into . . . any of the native dialects. I realized . . . that the task of making an English-speaking race of these Natives was much easier than the task of making a civilized and Christian language out of the Native languages. We should let the old tongues with their superstitions and sin die—the sooner the better—and replace these languages with that of Christian civilization, and compel the Natives in our schools to speak English and English only." Along with the native languages, these schools often tried to suppress Orthodoxy. Students were encouraged to choose an "American" rather than a "Russian" religion, and Orthodox priests were not allowed to administer the sacraments to them. The only religious instruction allowed was according to Protestant principles.

True to the tradition of speaking up for the helpless that the original missionaries had brought to Alaska, Orthodox church leaders protested against the policies of Jackson and his associates. Church periodicals

A totem pole in Sitka commemorates a historic battle between the Russians (together with their Aleut allies) and the local Tlingit tribe. Despite such confrontations, the Tlingits eventually adopted Orthodoxy, in part because of its openness to native culture.

Orthodox vs. Protestant Missions

Following the sale of Alaska to the United States, Protestant missionaries energetically pursued programs intended to Americanize the Orthodox native peoples. In response, the American Orthodox Messenger *published articles like this one by the Alaskan Priest-Monk Dionysius (1901), in which the Orthodox approach to mission is contrasted with the political and cultural approach taken by many Western Christians.*

If then our Orthodox Russian foreign missions are entirely spiritual, it follows that they are not, and cannot be, *political* in character. They never did, and do not now strive for the acquisition of power or influence in political affairs. They do not look on the propagation of Christianity as merely a means for the subjugation of heathens under the power of the Russian government. All this is the business of the State and its diplomatic missions—not of the Church and her evangelizing staff. And history shows that only those evangelizers successfully plied their task of converting heathens to Christ, who pursued purely spiritual objects, aimed only at the heathens' spiritual welfare, without admixture of any political scheming whatsoever. . . .

Our foreign missions, then, are distinctly not of a political nature. But neither do they aim at a *cultural* character. They do not understand their tasks in the sense of propagating European culture and civilization among savage peoples—in the sense of imparting to foreign races useful knowledge, handicrafts and the like—and never have they set cultural problems in the place of their own proper spiritual tasks. The reason for this, of course, is that European culture and civilization are by no means, as so many fancy, wholly an outgrowth of Christianity. European culture owes to Christianity only the little that is really noble and lofty in it;—if we go into particulars, we shall find that it is in direct opposition to it. The two are frequently two contrasting realms, two wholly different worlds. The one—all love, meekness, humility, renunciation of all that is of earth, and hope of an eternal life in heaven. The other—composed of self-love, sensuality, extreme egotism, complete attachment to earth, tending wholly to man's utter enslavement to earth by the witchery of the earthly comforts it keeps inventing, aiming at making him not one having dominion over this visible world (Gn 1:28), but a servant of it, ready to sacrifice for its sake all that is most sacred. It is self-evident from this that a mixing of spiritual with cultural aims, and, still more, a substitution of the latter for the former in a mission's work, must lead to most deplorable results. Religious missions pursuing cultural aims make of native converts, at the best, sensible, thrifty people, craftsmen, tradesmen,—men, it may be, useful to the state in a certain sense, hardy and enduring in the struggle for existence—but in no way Christians, loving, suffering, contented with their lot and ready to give up even the little they have, for Christ's sake. At the worst, they turn out idlers, sharpers, while natives that have made money develop into taskmasters who grind down their own people. . . .

It follows that our foreign mission work stands outside of and above all political and narrowly cultural aims, and pursues the exclusive task of propagating the kingdom of God upon earth. In this lies its success, its power, the pledge of its vitality and duration. Very poor in material means, scant in numbers, inconspicuous by their humble external organization and the absence of striking effects, *our missions are strong by the divine spirit which animates them, their internal warmth of feeling,* and succeed where it is least to be expected they should, judging from merely human probabilities and calculations.

Sitka residents perform a traditional native dance in a parish celebration. Respect for native culture and traditions has helped to maintain Orthodoxy as an important element in Alaskan life.

published articles denouncing abuses, and concerned churchmen sent petitions to federal officials in Washington. In 1898 Bishop Nicholas Ziorov, head of the Russian North American diocese, addressed a sharp letter to President McKinley in which he appealed for protection from officials who were "sent to Alaska without any discrimination and exclusively on the recommendation of Alaska's immovable guardian, Sheldon Jackson." He continued, "Alaska must be delivered from that man. By his sectarian propaganda he has introduced dissension, enmity and iniquity where those evils did not before exist. It was the Orthodox Church which brought the light of truth to that country; why then try to drive her out of it by every means, lawful or unlawful?"

Unfortunately, such protests did not succeed in stopping the abusive practices. In fact, they prompted even sharper attacks on the Orthodox church. In its coverage of the letter to President McKinley, the *New York Tribune* denounced Bishop Nicholas for his "blind and unwarranted prejudice against this Protestant country and its excellent schools." Sheldon

Jackson also reacted angrily, warning that the "days of the Orthodox Church are numbered" and that "twenty-five years from now, there will not be any Orthodox Church members left in Alaska." But Jackson underestimated the resilience of Orthodoxy in Alaska—a resilience that was the direct result of its approach to mission. As articles in the *American Orthodox Messenger* at the time noted, Orthodox missions do not try to promote a political agenda or impose a particular culture. Rather, they are open to all cultures.

Its openness to native culture allowed the Orthodox mission in Alaska to succeed, while Jackson's assimilationist policies only turned the native peoples away. For example, at first the Tlingit Indians of southeastern Alaska showed little interest in Orthodoxy. But in the 1880s, under mounting pressures from Jackson's associates, their leaders asked the Orthodox bishop for teachers and clergy and encouraged their people to accept baptism in the Orthodox church. As these Tlingit leaders recognized, by accepting Orthodoxy the Alaskans could maintain their cultural identity. A century after Jackson's angry prediction that it would soon vanish, the Orthodox church in Alaska remains alive and strong. It has survived because, from its very beginnings, it was envisioned as an Alaskan church.

Chapter 3

A Church
of Immigrants

By the 1860s Orthodoxy had become a significant part of the culture of the native peoples of Alaska, but in the mainland United States it had made very little impact. Consular officials, shipping agents, and merchants from Greece and Russia provided an Orthodox presence in a handful of port cities, but organized church life was only beginning. Orthodoxy seemed destined to remain on the fringes of American life. Within a few decades, however, this situation changed dramatically. Beginning in the late 1880s, a growing tide of immigration from Eastern Europe, the Balkans, and the Middle East made Orthodoxy one of the fastest-growing faiths in America.

One of the first Orthodox parishes in the continental United States was organized in New Orleans in 1864 by a group of Greek cotton traders under the direction of Nicholas Benakis, the local consul of the kingdom of Greece. Like other parishes before the period of mass immigration, this Eastern Orthodox Church of the Holy Trinity was multiethnic, with Russian, Serbian, and Arab members as well as Greeks. Services were conducted in English, Church Slavonic, and Greek, and as late as 1906, official records were kept in English rather than Greek. In certain respects, this parish was an early example of what would become common in the following decades, particularly in Greek communities: there was no supervision by a bishop. According to Orthodox canon law,

The Eastern Orthodox Church of the Holy Trinity in New Orleans, Louisiana, was organized by a group of Greek cotton merchants in 1864 to serve the city's small, multiethnic Orthodox community. It is considered to be the oldest Greek Orthodox parish in the United States.

a parish is not an independent entity. The bishop of the diocese or some other ecclesiastical superior must bless its establishment and assign its clergy. But in the 1860s New Orleans was far from any of the traditional centers of Orthodoxy. Needing a priest for the new parish, Benakis and the other members of the community's board of trustees contacted the Greek consul general in New York City. It happened that a well-educated Orthodox priest of Ukrainian background, Father Agapios Honcharenko, had just arrived in New York, having fled Europe to avoid harassment and possible assassination at the hands of Russian agents for his involvement in anti-czarist activities. Father Honcharenko spoke Greek well and had become a Greek citizen two years earlier. He was a convenient and obvious choice to become the New Orleans parish's first priest.

In the same year that the New Orleans parish was organized, a group of 16 Orthodox Christians in San Francisco, including the Greek and Russian consuls, met to form the Greek-Russian-Slavic Church and Philanthropic Society. After receiving a state charter in 1867, the society petitioned the Holy Synod of the Russian Orthodox church to assign a priest to the parish. The Holy Synod responded by transferring a priest and cantor from the cathedral in Sitka, Alaska, and grant-ng an annual cash subsidy to support them. In addition, the Russian czar made a substantial contribution toward construction of the church building. An energetic new bishop in Alaska, John Mitropolsky, was quick to recognize San Francisco's strategic importance for the future of Orthodoxy in America. The city was headquarters for the U.S. occupation authorities that now governed Alaska and the major port for transportation to and from that territory. Bishop John reasoned that he could more effectively defend the interests of the Alaskan mission from San Francisco than from Alaska itself. In addition, he saw that the city could serve as a base for expanding the activities of the mission to include the continental United States. In 1870 he asked the Holy Synod to authorize transfer of the diocesan headquarters from Sitka to San Francisco. In 1872 the Holy Synod approved his request. Two years later the bishop, the mission school, and the diocesan administration moved into the new cathedral of St. Alexander Nevsky on San Francisco's Russian Hill.

Even before the official transfer of the diocesan headquarters to San Francisco, the Russian mission in North America was expanding in new directions. In 1864 a representative of the Protestant Episcopal church in the United States had urged the Russian Orthodox church to establish a center or "showplace" where Americans could learn about Orthodoxy firsthand. Nothing came of this proposal until 1870, when Nicholas Bjerring, a professor of philosophy and church history at St. Mary's Seminary in Baltimore, left the Roman Catholic church and asked to be received into the Orthodox church. (Bjerring was one of a number of prominent Roman Catholics who disagreed with the dogma of papal infallibility set forth at the First Vatican Council in 1869–70. According to this dogma, the pope is always and absolutely right when he solemnly and officially defines a matter of faith or morals.) After Bjerring was ordained to the priesthood in St. Petersburg, he was assigned to establish a church in New York City. From his little "Greek-Russian church" (located in the parlor of his home) he ministered to a small but diverse flock of consular personnel and assorted Orthodox residents of the city.

Bjerring spent most of his time publishing works in English relating to Orthodoxy. In addition to translations of virtually all the liturgical services of the Orthodox church, he produced the *Oriental Church Magazine*, whose purpose was "to lay before English-speaking readers a candid and authoritative statement of the constitution, tenets, and progress of the Oriental Church, which are so little known and understood in the Western Continent, except by that limited circle of students which makes the study of the religion of mankind a special study." Bjerring's work is in certain ways similar to Bishop Innocent Veniaminov's efforts to prepare texts in the native languages of Alaska—but if Bjerring's goal was to convert significant numbers of mainstream Americans to Orthodoxy, he was not very successful. His records for 1870–80 indicate that during that period

A group of Carpatho-Russian immigrants gather for a portrait in national costume. In America, the church gave immigrants a way to maintain Old World traditions not just in religion but also in music, folk dancing, poetry, and food.

he performed 53 baptisms, 12 weddings, and 14 burials, but received only 4 converts into the Orthodox church.

In San Francisco the administrators of the Russian diocese also took an interest in using English to advance the work of the North American mission. Bishop Vladimir Sokolovsky combined his linguistic ability with musical talent to create English-language settings for the most common Russian liturgical chants. In addition, he appointed an "English preacher" for the cathedral: Father Sebastian Dabovich, the first Orthodox priest born in the United States. The diocesan administration also tried to minister to the small, scattered, and ethnically diverse North American flock by recruiting priests who spoke many languages. Father Dabovich, who was of Serbian parentage, organized the first predominantly Serbian

Orthodox church in the country, in Jackson, California (1894). He also served in several of the multiethnic parishes the diocese established in the course of the 1880s and 1890s. Russian-educated Greek priests such as Father Theoklitos Triantafilidis and Michael Andreades served in the handful of diocesan parishes that had large Greek populations, and Russian-educated Syro-Arab priests such as Father Raphael Hawaweeny organized church life for the growing Middle Eastern community. But the character of Orthodoxy in America—and the character of America itself—was changing rapidly. Massive immigration was transforming what had begun as a small mission *to* America into a large but fragmented collection of ethnic parishes intent on giving newcomers a shelter *from* America.

In the half-century between 1870 and 1920, around 27 million immigrants entered the United States. In the early years most were from the northern European nations that had supplied earlier waves of immigration, but by the end of this period the majority of immigrants were coming from southern, central, and eastern Europe. Many of these "new immigrants," as they have been called, were Eastern Christians. Like their Roman Catholic and Jewish counterparts, they differed from earlier immigrant groups in several ways. Nearly half were illiterate. Virtually none was trained in a profession or craft. Though most came from farming villages, they found work in the United States mainly in the cities and industrial centers. The vast majority were young single males who wanted to earn enough money in America to return to their home countries and enjoy a good life—a Romanian saying was, "A thousand dollars and home." These immigrants did not intend to stay permanently in America. As a result, many acquired only a rudimentary knowledge of English and of American ways. Even when they sent home for a wife and extended their stay indefinitely, they lived on the fringes of a society that tolerated their presence only because they were a cheap source of labor.

New York City was the new immigrants' usual port of entry. From there they dispersed to the industrial centers of the northeast, seeking out relatives or compatriots who could help them find work. They met in

text continues on page 61

It Happened in Elmira

The "new immigrants" who entered the United States around the turn of the century cooperated with each other in various ways to meet the challenges of life in the New World, but they often ended up disagreeing about religious allegiances. A parish priest named Father Samuel Sulich summarizes the recollections of "old-timers" from Holy Trinity Orthodox Church, Elmira, New York. The Ukrainian church he refers to on page 59 was Eastern Catholic, or Uniate. Eventually those within the parish who identified themselves as "Russian" organized their own brotherhood and their own church within the North American Archdiocese of the Russian Orthodox church, which was then headed by Archbishop Evdokim Meshchersky.

A priest from Binghamton came only once or twice a month for services on Sunday in Elmira Heights in 1910. Tekla Obuhanych and her fiancé wanted to get married, but the priest had a problem—he had to leave for Binghamton the next morning on the 7:00 A.M. train. He told them and another couple to be at the railroad station in Elmira Heights at 6:00 A.M. and he would marry them before departing on the only train to Binghamton. Both couples agreed and were married at the railroad station at 6:00 A.M.

People came to Elmira Heights from Austria-Hungary and were lured to the area by factories and promises of employment. They were very young when they arrived and the main employment for the men was at the iron works, foundries and the U.S. Steel Bridge Works. The women worked in the textile mills. The immigrants did not find it hard to get employment at these places, for they worked very hard, long hours for very little pay—10¢ an hour, $6.00 per week. It was every man's dream to work at the Bicycle Shop, the Eclipse-Bendix Corporation, inasmuch as the work was not as difficult and wages were a bit higher, up to $8.00 per week. To be hired by Eclipse upon arrival was next to impossible, for they did not hire "greenhorns." The first immigrant to be hired by Eclipse was Mr. Kuryla, a member of the church. He in turn asked for a job for his friend, who in turn asked for some more friends, and finally there were many immigrants working at this plant. . . .

The salary did not go far for most men and women. Single men paid $3.00 per month for room and board, which included laundry and a lunch pail. Women paid $2.00 because they did their own laundry. Three men slept while three others worked the night shift. When the night shift men returned home in the morning, those who occupied the bedroom at night were off to work and the beds were used day and night. Married couples who rented a house for $4.00 a month would often rent bedrooms to other married couples for $3.00 with kitchen privileges, and thereby earn money. . . .

Originally, all the Slavic-speaking people in the area attended the same church (Ukrainian) located on 14th Street in Elmira Heights. It should be mentioned that the town is separated by two sets of railroad tracks. In 1907 or 1908, property was purchased on Horseheads Boulevard and the church was literally moved across 14th Street to the new location. When the church was moved as far as the Erie Railroad tracks, funds were needed to pay the utility company to cut the electric wires. Since there were no funds, the church was left there for some weeks until the people of the parish collected the money. In the meantime,

continued on next page

continued from previous page

temporary steps were placed in front of the church and services were held on the spot for several weeks. When the money was collected, the wires were cut and the church was moved to the D.L.&W. tracks, where the same situation occurred. Again the temporary steps were placed in front of the church and services held there until the money was raised to cut the wires. Finally the church was moved to its new location on Horseheads Boulevard.

In about 1916, there was a rift between the Ukrainian and Russian factions in the church. Early in 1916, a small group of Russian men who had been organized as the Sts. Peter and Paul Brotherhood met at the home of Andrew Basal to discuss the problem, and eventually the Holy Trinity Russian Orthodox Church was organized. Upon request of the committee, Archbishop Evdokim sent Father Borisoff to assist the twenty-five families in organizing the parish. Plans were established for the erection of a church. A few weeks later Father Borisoff reported that Father Timothy Berkey was to come to Elmira as pastor. But now the young committee was embarrassed, for there was no housing for a priest and his family. Everyone was willing to sacrifice, however, and Kozma Mowchan offered his home for the Sunday liturgy and the housing of the pastor and his family. So for the next four weeks, the Russian Orthodox Divine Liturgy in Elmira was held in the home of Kozma Mowchan on McCauley Avenue. Soon the new church was completed and gradually outfitted for services.

text continued from page 57

rooming houses, saloons, and coffee houses to discuss the latest news from home. They formed social clubs and patriotic organizations in order to maintain a sense of cultural identity. They organized mutual aid societies and brotherhoods for support in times of distress and need. And quickly enough they set about establishing parish churches. The new immigrants were not necessarily deeply religious people, but in their home countries religion had been a part of life. As one immigrant put it, "there couldn't be any Greek life"—or Serbian life or Russian life or Romanian life—"without the church."

Creation of these parishes typically proceeded without formal approval or material support from church authorities. Members of a community would raise money to buy land and construct a church building or, more often, to purchase an existing building from another group that already had moved up the socioeconomic ladder. Only then would they ask a bishop, usually one from their home region across the sea, to send them a priest. In this way immigrant groups established hundreds of parishes in which they were free to express their pride in their social, cultural, linguistic, and spiritual heritage. But almost inevitably these parishes tended to become closed ethnic enclaves, with little interest in wider Orthodox unity and little sense of mission. Had these new immigrants been aware of the English-language publications Father Nicholas Bjerring had prepared a few decades earlier, they would have had little appreciation for them. They were more interested in preserving church life as they had known it in their villages in the Old World.

But the new American parishes differed from those of the Old World in an important way—they often had a keen sense of their independence from outside supervision by church authorities. With little knowledge of Orthodox canon law but great awareness of how most American Protestants organized their church life, the immigrants emphasized the independence of the local parish. Control typically was in the hands of a board of trustees elected from among the more prominent laymen of the community. The priest was regarded as an employee of the parish corporation, and the board of trustees could dismiss him if he did not meet its expectations.

The first large-scale immigration of Eastern Christians to the United States came from the Austro-Hungarian Empire, from the Carpathian mountain regions that today are divided among Poland, Slovakia, Hungary, Moldova, and Ukraine. These people were known by various names: Carpatho-Russians, Ruthenians, Rusyns, Uhro-Rusyns (if they came from Hungary), Galicians (if they came from those areas of Poland then ruled by Austria), or Trans-Carpathian Ukrainians. Originally Eastern Orthodox Christians, they had entered into the Roman Catholic church through a series of "unions" in the late 16th and 17th centuries, under pressure from the Catholic rulers of Poland and Austria-Hungary. These "Uniates" (as the Orthodox called them) or "Greek Catholics" (as the Catholics called them) retained their Eastern forms of worship and many Eastern customs and practices—for example, priests could be married. Their bishops, however, were under the authority of Rome. For simple Carpathian villagers in Europe, their hybrid "Uniate" status made little difference. They continued to call themselves *Pravoslavny*, Orthodox, to distinguish themselves from the neighboring Slovak, Polish, and Hungarian Latin Catholics. In America, however, their church status would become a major source of controversy.

From the late 1870s onward, Carpatho-Russian peasants streamed into the United States. By 1917 they numbered more than 350,000. Many went to the coal-mining regions of Pennsylvania, where they replaced striking German, Welsh, and Irish miners. They received a cool welcome. At the time, many native-born Americans were opposed to immigration and resented the willingness of these aliens to work for as little as 10 cents an hour. American Catholic bishops were hardly more sympathetic. Most of these bishops were ignorant of the many historical, cultural, linguistic, and liturgical features that distinguished the Greek Catholics from Latin Catholic immigrants. As a result, the bishops opposed the creation of specifically Greek Catholic parishes. Their thinking ran: If these people really are good Catholics, let them attend the existing Latin Catholic churches of their Slovak, Polish, and Hungarian neighbors!

Despite the American bishops' opposition, the Carpatho-Russian immigrants went ahead and organized parishes on their own, then wrote to the Greek Catholic bishops in their home countries requesting priests. When these priests arrived, however, the American bishops refused to accept their credentials and regarded them as schismatics, or people who had wrongfully separated themselves from the church. The Greek Catholic priests continued to serve their immigrant flocks anyway, relying on the blessing given to them by their bishops in Europe. Mutual distrust and hostility increased, causing many Greek Catholics to question the very basis of their union with the Roman church.

The Carpatho-Russians' struggle to maintain their religious and cultural identity in the face of Latin hostility soon took a new form. In 1889 Father Alexis Toth, a widowed Greek Catholic priest, arrived in Minneapolis, Minnesota, to serve at the newly established St. Mary's Greek Catholic church. Toth knew that he was supposed to present his credentials to the local Catholic bishop in order to receive permission to serve in his new assignment, but his interview with Archbishop John Ireland did not go at all well. Ireland strongly believed in the Americanization of Catholic immigrants and had little sympathy for the Carpatho-Russians and others who resisted assimilation and clung to their European religious traditions. Ireland refused to accept Toth as a regularly ordained priest and forbade local Catholics to have any dealings with him.

Soon after this encounter, Toth and seven other Greek Catholic priests met to coordinate strategies for dealing with hostile American bishops such as Ireland. Because they had held the meeting without permission from church authorities, Rome ordered them back to Europe. Deeply discouraged, Toth told his parishioners that under the circumstances, the best course of action would be for him to leave them. But, as he later recounts, the parishioners were reluctant to lose their new priest and declared, "No, let's go to the Russian bishop. Why should we always submit ourselves to foreigners?" "All right," replied Toth, "but where does the Russian bishop live? And what is his name?" Toth learned that there was indeed a Russian bishop in America, that he lived in San Francisco,

Father Alexis Toth blesses Easter baskets at St. Mary's Church in Minneapolis, Minnesota. One of the reasons why this large Carpatho-Russian community decided to enter Orthodoxy was their attachment to their Eastern Christian religious and cultural heritage.

and that his name was His Grace Bishop Vladimir. The parish decided to send two of its members to investigate. They returned with a welcome gift of icons for their church. After a round of correspondence, Father Toth traveled to San Francisco. Shortly thereafter, on March 25, 1891, Bishop Vladimir traveled to Minneapolis to receive the entire community of 361 parishioners into the Orthodox church. The "return of the Unia" had begun.

The energetic Toth soon was crisscrossing the northeastern United States to encourage other Carpatho-Russians to return to the church of their forebears. By the time of his death in 1909, he had led 65 communities with some 20,000 parishioners back to Orthodoxy. Realizing too late what was going on, Rome tried to stem the tide of defections by sending a Greek Catholic bishop, Soter Ortinsky, to the United States in 1907. However, Rome undercut this gesture by issuing, in that same year, a decree that limited Eastern Catholic rights. Despite Rome's efforts, the movement that Toth had begun gained momentum. By 1917, some 163 Carpatho-Russian communities with more than 100,000 faithful had entered the Russian missionary diocese.

This "return of the Unia" profoundly transformed the missionary diocese, giving it a new orientation and a new character as well as thousands of new members. When its leaders moved the diocesan headquarters from Alaska to San Francisco, they could hardly have imagined that their struggling mission to mainstream America would achieve its first major success with the mass conversion of Uniate immigrants. The diocese now faced several new challenges. It needed to ensure that multitudes of former Uniates would become fully integrated into the church and, if possible, to reach out to others who might want to join. How could the diocese do this in a way that would not look as though it were simply trying to make them into Russians? It had to meet the spiritual needs of the many other Orthodox immigrant groups—Arabs, Serbs, Greeks, Albanians, Romanians, Bulgarians—now beginning to stream into the United States. How could the diocese ensure the structural unity of Orthodoxy in America while at the same time respecting the wide variety of languages, customs, and forms of worship that these groups held dear? And if it was to be true to its original missionary vocation, it needed to become more visible in mainstream American religious life. How then was Orthodoxy to be integrated into American life without giving up the rich cultural heritage that it had received from Europe and the Middle East?

The ruling bishops of this period—Nicholas Ziorov (1891–98), Tikhon Bellavin (1898–1907), Platon Rozhdestvensky (1907–14 and 1922–34), and Evdokim Meshchersky (1914–17)—addressed these challenges in a variety of ambitious ways. Through their combined efforts, the North American mission by 1917 would include more than 350 parishes and chapels, a seminary, a women's vocational training school, a monastery and a convent, an orphanage, an immigrant aid society, and a savings bank, with a projected annual central administrative budget of more than a quarter of a million dollars.

Father Alexis Toth Encounters Archbishop John Ireland

December 19, 1889, was a turning point in the history of Orthodoxy in America. Alexis Toth, then an Eastern Catholic or Uniate priest, went to the local Roman Catholic archbishop, John Ireland, seeking permission to serve a newly formed parish of Carpatho-Russians in Minneapolis, Minnesota. Ireland's refusal sparked a massive "return of the Unia" to Orthodoxy. In an article written later for the newspaper of the Russian Orthodox North American Diocese, Toth gives his account of what happened on that day.

The place of my appointment was Minneapolis, Minnesota, in the diocese of Archbishop John Ireland. As an obedient Uniate, I complied with the orders of my bishop [the bishop of Presov], who at that time was John Valiy, and appeared before Bishop Ireland on December 19, 1889. I kissed his hand, as I should have, according to custom (failing, however, to kneel before him, which as I learned later was my chief mistake), and presented my credentials. I remember well that no sooner did he read that I was a "Greek Catholic" than his hands began to shake! It took him almost 15 minutes to read to the end, after which he asked me abruptly (the conversation was in the Latin language):

"Do you have a wife?"

"No."

"But you had one?"

"Yes. I am a widower."

Hearing this, he threw the paper on the table and loudly shouted: "I have already written to Rome protesting against this kind of priest being sent to me."

"What kind of priest do you mean?"

"Your kind."

"But I am a Catholic priest of the Greek rite. I am a Uniate, and I was ordained by a lawful Catholic bishop."

"I do not consider that either you or that bishop are Catholic. Besides, I do not need any Greek Catholic priests here. A Polish priest in Minneapolis is more than enough. He can also be the priest for the Greeks."

"But he belongs to the Latin Rite. Besides, our people will not understand him and so they will hardly go to him. That was the reason that they built a church of their own."

John Ireland, himself an Irish immigrant, became the Catholic Archbishop of St. Paul, Minnesota in 1888, and he strongly encouraged Catholic migration to the state.

"I did not give them permission to do that, and I do not grant you jurisdiction to serve here."

I was deeply hurt by this kind of fanaticism of this representative of papal Rome and sharply replied to him: "In that case I neither ask from you a jurisdiction nor your permission. I know the rights of my church. I know the basis on which the Unia was established, and I will act according to them."

The archbishop lost his temper. I lost mine just as much. One word led to another. The thing went so far that it is not worthwhile to reconstruct our entire conversation further.

Archbishop (later Patriarch) Tikhon Bellavin was one of the most energetic leaders of the young American archdiocese in the years preceding the Communist revolution in Russia.

Of these bishops, certainly the most beloved and most influential was Tikhon. Thirty-three years old at the time of his arrival in the United States, he was one of the youngest bishops in the Russian Orthodox church. During his time in America the missionary diocese was transformed into a multiethnic archdiocese with a growing array of programs and projects. After his return to Russia, he became in quick succession Archbishop of Jaroslavl, Archbishop of Vilnius, Metropolitan of Moscow, and—in the midst of the Communist revolution of 1917—the first Patriarch of Moscow and All Russia in more than 200 years. Subjected to constant harassment and persecution by the Communists, he died while under house arrest in 1925. With the fall of communism in 1989, the Russian Orthodox church formally canonized him as a saint. But long before that he was recognized as one of the 20th century's greatest witnesses to the Christian faith.

On arriving in the United States, Tikhon made a series of pastoral visits throughout his far-flung diocese. He was struck by the need for more effective ways to minister to his multiethnic flock. In 1903 he requested that an auxiliary, or assistant, bishop be ordained specifically for Alaska, in view of its special needs. The following year, in the first ordination of an Orthodox bishop ever performed in the New World, Tikhon and his Alaskan auxiliary ordained a second auxiliary, Raphael Hawaweeny, to have responsibility specifically for Arab Orthodox immigrants. This was no small task. Unlike most other Orthodox immigrant groups, the Arabs had spread out thinly across the continent rather than clustering in a few cities and regions. As a priest, Father Hawaweeny had distinguished himself by his efforts to seek them out wherever they happened to be. As a bishop, he would travel even more widely and supplement this personal contact with a monthly magazine called *al-Kalimat* (The Word).

In 1905 the work of reorganization continued. Tikhon raised Father Sebastian Dabovich to the rank of archimandrite, or abbot, with responsibility specifically for Serbian immigrants. He also received permission to transfer the diocesan headquarters from San Francisco to New York City, where it would be closer to the new immigrant parishes of the industrial northeast, and was honored with the title of archbishop. That same year, in a report to the Holy Synod of the Russian Orthodox church, Tikhon set forth his vision for the church in America. He observed that "the diocese is not only multinational: It is composed of several Orthodox churches, which keep the unity of the faith but preserve their peculiarities in canonical structure, in liturgical rules, in parish life. These peculiarities are dear to them and can perfectly well be tolerated in the pan-Orthodox scene. We do not consider that we have the right to suppress the national character of the churches here. On the contrary, we try to preserve this character, and we confer on them the latitude to be governed by leaders of their own nationality." After pointing out arrangements already made for the Arab Orthodox, Tikhon proposed the creation of distinct auxiliary dioceses for the Serbs (under Dabovich) and other major national groups in America. The church as whole would continue to be headed by the Russian archbishop, but in view of the fact that "life in the New World is different from that in the Old . . . , a greater autonomy, and possibly autocephaly [ecclesiastical independence], should be granted to the church in America."

While Tikhon was attentive to the needs of the various Orthodox ethnic groups in America, he also recognized that their life there inevitably would be different from the life they had known before. The archdiocese would have to adapt itself to the American context. The key to success, in

Tikhon's estimation, was a knowledge of the English language and familiarity with American ways. In his annual reports to the Holy Synod in Russia, he often spoke of the need for liturgical and educational materials in the English language, particularly in view of "the ever-growing interest among the Americans in the Orthodox faith." He also pointed out "how beneficial and necessary it is for our missionaries here to acquire skill in the English language, since they have to preach and conduct the divine services in it." Priests on temporary assignment from Russia, he observed, were seldom adequately equipped for ministry in America. At the very least, they needed an opportunity to "acclimatize." Even more necessary, in his estimation, was a seminary where young people born in America could "study and become pastors for the people from within their own milieu, knowing their spirit, customs and language." To meet these needs, in 1905 Tikhon established a North American Ecclesiastical Seminary, which was eventually located in Tenafly, New Jersey, for training future clergy. He also established a monastery in South Canaan, Pennsylvania, named for his patron, St. Tikhon of Zadonsk, where missionary monks could come for reflection and revitalization.

The development of educational and charitable institutions within the archdiocese continued after Tikhon returned to Russia, but his innovative plan for ethnic auxiliary dioceses was never fully put into action. The bishops who followed him directed much of their attention to the "return of the Unia." With the approach of World War I, which would pit the Russian Empire against the Austro-Hungarian Empire, struggles for the allegiance of the Carpatho-Russians became increasingly bitter. Often political considerations and Russian patriotism overshadowed religious concerns.

In the face of such concern over the Uniates, the diocese somewhat neglected the Balkan Slavs, Arabs, Greeks, and other Orthodox groups. Under the leadership of Bishop Raphael Hawaweeny, the Arabs had shown that it was possible to maintain ethnic identity within a united Orthodox church in America. But after his death in 1915, a visiting bishop from the Patriarchate of Antioch tried to become the leader of the

Arab parishes. Although the patriarchate announced that it did not support his actions, he and his supporters—the "Antacky," or pro-Antiochians—soon began to clash with the "Russy," or pro-Russians, who remained loyal to Raphael's assistant and eventual successor within the Russian North American archdiocese, Bishop Aftimios Ofiesh.

The Serbs also were restless. An assembly of 12 parishes in 1913 expressed dissatisfaction with their position in the North American archdiocese and voted to join the Serbian Orthodox church in Belgrade instead. Belgrade did not respond, and the matter was shelved for the time being. But the decision of the Serbian parishes, like the Arab clash between "Antacky" and "Russy," did not bode well for the continued organizational unity of Orthodoxy in America.

Most problematic was the status of the growing number of Greek parishes in the United States. Since the 1890s Greek immigrants from the Ottoman Turkish Empire and the kingdom of Greece had streamed into the United States, spurred by oppression at the hands of the Turks, poor economic conditions at home, and exaggerated reports of opportunities in America. Between 1890 and 1910, approximately 300,000 Greeks arrived, most after 1905. Between 1910 and 1920, another 300,000 joined them. Like many other "new immigrants," most of them did not plan to stay permanently. As many as half returned to the land of their birth one or more times. Those who did stay tended to concentrate in urban areas, where they often set up small businesses—candy shops, shoeshine stands, restaurants. Major cities like Chicago soon had bustling "Greek towns," where recent arrivals could enjoy a measure of psychological as well as economic security and a refuge from widespread anti-immigrant feelings. In these urban ethnic communities, in classic "new immigrant" fashion, the Greeks quickly organized social clubs, mutual aid societies, and parishes. Although these parishes were quite independent of any diocesan authority, they were dependent on the political and regional preferences of their members.

The first such parish was established in New York City in 1892, when about 500 Greeks, many from around Athens, met to form the Society of

Athena. Soon they had collected enough money and pledges to build a church and ask the Holy Synod of the Church of Greece to send a priest. A few months later Father Paisios Ferentinos arrived to begin services for the new Holy Trinity parish. After a short time, however, disagreement erupted between the parish's board of trustees and the Society of Athena. A dissatisfied group wrote to the Patriarchate of Constantinople, rather than to the Holy Synod of Greece, asking for "an educated priest." The patriarchate sent Father Callinikos Dilbaes to serve the breakaway group's newly formed Annunciation parish.

A similar chain of events led to the formation of two independent Greek parishes in Chicago. By 1892 the Greeks there had formed the Society of Lycurgos, which in turn organized the Annunciation parish and obtained a priest from the Holy Synod of the Church of Greece. The Society of Lycurgos, named for the famous lawgiver of ancient Sparta, was dominated by immigrants from that city, and their chosen priest hailed from the same region. But the society also included a growing number of immigrants from the rival region of Arcadia. In 1897 a group of these Arcadians went off to fight in the Greco-Turkish war. They arrived too late for the war, but while in Greece they met a priest from Arcadia who was eager to visit his two sons in Chicago. With a congenial priest so readily available, the Chicago Arcadians quickly established a parish of their own.

The beautiful interior of St. Nicholas Greek Orthodox Cathedral in Tarpon Springs, Florida. The parish was originally organized by immigrant sponge fishermen from Greece.

As these examples suggest, the early Greek parishes formed and functioned with little or no supervision by bishops. In practice they were independent of any authority beyond the local community. Some might ask the Church of Greece to supply a priest, while others turned to the patriarchates of Constantinople, Alexandria, or Jerusalem. Some simply relied on the recommendations of friends and relatives back home. It is little wonder that a few parishes were misled into hiring impostors, usually vagrant monks who pretended to be ordained priests in order to obtain money for performing marriages, baptisms, and other church rites. But whatever arrangements were made, the lay board of trustees continued to view itself as the ultimate authority within the parish.

The Russian archdiocese in North America did make some attempts to minister to the Greek "new immigrants." Several Greek priests served in the diocese's multiethnic parishes, particularly in the western states. Sometimes the diocese provided icons and liturgical articles to Greek parishes. In Chicago in 1902, Bishop Tikhon even celebrated the Divine Liturgy (the eucharistic service of the Orthodox church) in an independent Greek parish—entirely in Greek. On the other hand, when he attempted to serve in a parish in New York City in 1904, he was barred from entering by its angry trustees, who feared a Russian takeover of their parish properties.

But Greek fears alone do not account for the failure of the Orthodox in America to reach a higher degree of unity in this period. Indifference and neglect on the part of the church hierarchy also played a role. In a 1908 report to Archbishop Platon, one of his assistants pointed out the need for more participation of Greeks in the church administration. Platon agreed in principle, but he also expressed his doubts: "Although the idea of a united leadership is so really important for the success of Orthodoxy in America ... it seems it is not feasible, if one takes into account the traditional self-sufficiency of the Greeks in questions of religion and faith.... The Greeks here do not contact the Russian bishops. At least I have not seen a Greek at my place during the four months of my stay here." Clearly, Archbishop Platon was no more inclined to seek out the Greeks than they were to seek out him.

Descent of the Holy Spirit Romanian Orthodox Church in Gary, Indiana, was constructed in 1910. Like so many immigrant parishes, Holy Spirit was effectively independent for the first decades of its existence.

Greek fears? Official indifference and neglect? While these things did come into play, there is an overriding, and simpler, explanation for the declining concern for unity. The new immigrant groups—Greeks and Russians, but also Arabs, Serbs, Bulgarians, Albanians, Ukrainians, and Romanians—now made up the overwhelming majority of Orthodox Christians in America. And these people found it reassuring and altogether natural to associate with others of their ethnic group, and perhaps threatening and unnatural to associate with members of other ethnic groups. This was true whether their parishes were fully integrated into the Russian North American diocese or independent, as were most Greek parishes and those of several smaller ethnic groups. People within these groups knew that the other groups followed the same Orthodox faith and shared the same sacramental life, but they saw no overwhelming need to express this in organizational unity or practical cooperation. For the "new immigrants," the parishes they struggled so hard to establish were not just worshiping communities. They were also centers for social and cultural life. They protected and sustained the immigrants' world—their language, their customs, and their ties with the past, as well as their Orthodox Christian faith—in the face of a new society where even other Orthodox groups might seem to pose a threat.

The history of St. Spyridon Orthodox Church in Seattle, Washington, vividly illustrates the new Orthodox immigrants' tendency to divide along ethnic lines. The parish was founded in 1894 as part of the Russian North American diocese, but the first parishioners were predominantly Greek, and the church was named for a saint who was extremely popular in the

Greek Orthodox world but much less well known to Russians. For many years the parish was multiethnic, including Serbs, Carpatho-Russians, Bulgarians, Syrians, and gypsies as well as Greeks and Russians. Usually it was served by priests of the Russian diocese who spoke Greek, Russian, and English. But as the Orthodox population of Seattle grew, the Greek parishioners of St. Spyridon's began to think about establishing their own parish. In 1916 the Greek Community of Seattle was incorporated, and in time the corporation constructed a new church, named for St. Demetrios. Yet the division of what had been one parish seems to have aroused no hard feelings. The remaining parishioners of St. Spyridon expressed joy because "now there were enough Orthodox in Seattle for two churches." When the new parish formed, they escorted the Greek community in solemn procession to the new church. All parties seem to have considered it perfectly natural to organize church life along ethnic lines.

ДУХОВНЫЕ И СВѢТСКІЕ РЕВНИТЕЛИ ПРАВОСЛАВІЯ ВЪ С. АМЕРИКѢ
СО ВРЕМЕНИ ПЕРВАГО АЛЯСКИНСКАГО ЕПИСКОПА — ИННОКЕНТІЯ
ВЕНІАМИНОВА (1841 Г.) ПО НАШЕ ВРЕМЯ — 1937-Й Г.
КОМПОЗИЦІЯ СЕКРЕТАРЯ СОЮЗА ДУХОВЕНСТВА,
ПРОТ. ПЕТРА КОХАНИКА.

The Ethnic Churches

n a 1916 report to the Holy Synod of the Russian Orthodox church, Archbishop Evdokim Meshchersky was enthusiastic about the current state and future prospects of his North American archdiocese: "Have you encountered the same labor in your country? Have you seen the same rivers of gold which are poured out here by the private people and not by the government or state institutions? Have you seen such intense service rendered to those who suffer? Have you seen such multitudes of self-denying workers who voluntarily, without any pay, toil in Christ's vineyard?" After pointing out the growing strength of the archdiocese—and also the difficulties it encountered because it remained dependent on distant Russia—he concluded: "It is necessary to grant some kind of autocephaly to the mission"—in other words, to make the American branch of Orthodoxy an independent, or self-headed, body.

But the North American archdiocese was still quite dependent, both financially and administratively, on the Russian Orthodox church and on the empire to which that church was so closely linked. Until now that relationship had been advantageous for the North Americans, but after the 1917 Communist revolution in Russia, it became an overwhelming liability. The archdiocese was plunged into financial and administrative chaos. At the same time, the tendency toward ethnic separatism picked up speed. By 1940 there would be more than a dozen separate ecclesiastical "jurisdictions," or organizational structures, in North America, each organized along ethnic lines.

These jurisdictions brought a measure of order, unity, and pastoral care to groups that otherwise would have remained fragmented and enfeebled. At the same time, this restructuring of Orthodox church life carried with it a high price. Although the jurisdictions all claimed to profess the same faith and share the same sacraments, they had little contact with each other—and the little contact they did have was sometimes antagonistic. Orthodoxy in America lost any semblance of that visible, structural unity that Archbishop Tikhon had envisioned around the turn of the century.

The year 1917 was one of rapid change in Russia. In February, Czar Nicholas II yielded power to a provisional government. This gave the Russian Orthodox church an opportunity to pursue long-delayed plans for internal reform, and on August 15, the "All-Russian Council" convened in Moscow. When the Communists seized power in St. Petersburg on October 25, its deliberations continued. On October 31 the council decided to restore to the church the office of patriarch, which Czar Peter the Great had abolished nearly 200 years before. Five days later, Tikhon, former head of the North American archdiocese, was chosen for this awesome responsibility. But already the revolution had claimed its first clerical victim. On October 31 the Communists shot to death Father John Kochurov, who earlier had served as a mission priest in North America. He was the first of more than 12,000 clergy and 100,000 Orthodox Christians who the new rulers of Russia—soon to be known as the Soviet Union—would kill. By the end of the 1930s the Communists would have forcibly suppressed all of Russia's monasteries and seminaries, and fewer than 100 churches would remain open, mainly in order to show foreign visitors that there was "freedom of religion" in the Soviet Union.

One member of the All-Russian Council was Archbishop Evdokim. Before leaving North America for what everyone believed would be a brief absence, he had entrusted the administration of the archdiocese to one of his auxiliary bishops, Alexander Nemolovsky. But Archbishop

Evdokim never returned, and Bishop Alexander was forced to deal with financial and administrative problems far beyond his ability to solve.

Although Archbishop Evdokim had spoken in glowing terms about the prospects of his North American archdiocese in his 1916 report to the Holy Synod, most of the report had been about money. The archbishop had requested that the annual subsidy from Russia be increased from 89,930 rubles to 1,000,000. At the time the exchange rate was two rubles per U.S. dollar, and the dollar had approximately five times its present purchasing power. This means that in present-day dollars the archbishop was asking for a subsidy of $2,500,000! The Holy Synod agreed to a subsidy of 550,000 rubles ($275,000, or approximately $1,375,000 in present-day terms), but almost none of this money arrived. Bishop Alexander faced a financial crisis of major proportions. Not only were funds from Russia cut off. When Archbishop Evdokim left for Russia, the archdiocese had a debt of more than $100,000, and by 1919 this figure would almost double. Meanwhile, income plummeted. For 1922 receipts totaled only $2,557.

Like many people in both Russia and America, Bishop Alexander believed that the revolutionary tumult would be short-lived. He resorted to more loans and to mortgaging parish property, a move that was as unpopular among parishioners as it was unwise from a financial perspective. In 1922 the beleaguered bishop finally resigned and left the country, turning over administration of the archdiocese to Metropolitan Platon Rozhdestvensky, who previously had headed it (1907–14) and who now had returned to the United States as a refugee. The generosity of private benefactors helped stem the immediate financial crisis, but the archdiocese now faced a crisis of leadership. Who was to be acknowledged as its legitimate head? A council of archdiocesan clergy and church members, the "Third All-American Council," met in Pittsburgh in 1922. It proclaimed Platon as "Metropolitan of All America and Canada." He held that position until his death in 1934. Nevertheless, his authority was challenged from several directions.

The first and most ominous of these challenges had its roots in Russia. There, a group of "progressive" clergy, with the support of the new

Soviet regime, seized control of the headquarters of the Russian Orthodox church, declared Patriarch Tikhon deposed, and introduced many
changes to the liturgy (church services) and canon law (church disciplinary and administrative rules), including the ordination of married men
as bishops. This "Living Church" movement appointed an ex-priest who
earlier had served in America, John Kedrovsky, as its "metropolitan" for
America. Kedrovsky in turn tried to use the U.S. courts to gain control of
the parishes and other assets of the archdiocese, claiming to be its legiti-
mately appointed head. Faced with the threat of lawsuits, the archdiocese
began to return property deeds to individual parishes, undoing decades
of patient effort by bishops to maintain effective oversight and central
control. Many of the parishes introduced protective clauses into their
bylaws, such as: "No archbishop, metropolitan or bishop or any ecclesiastical authority of the North American Diocese shall have any authority,
claim or right to manage the real and personal estate of the corporation."
The bishop's authority was restricted to "spiritual-religious matters." This
meant that the archdiocese had no financial or administrative role in the
running of the parishes. In effect, it was reduced to a voluntary confeder-
ation of independent parishes.

While the struggle with the Living Church was mounting, communications with the legitimate patriarchal church in Russia were becoming
unreliable. Decrees bearing Patriarch Tikhon's signature showed every
sign of being issued under pressure, threats, or force. Unable to communicate freely with the patriarchal church and threatened by lawsuits
brought by Kedrovsky and the Living Church, the "Fourth All-American
Council," meeting in Detroit in 1924, proclaimed the North American
archdiocese to be "a temporarily self-governing church" until a future
council of the Russian Orthodox church could deal with ecclesiastical
affairs "under conditions of political freedom." From that time onward
the Russian Orthodox Greek Catholic Church of America, popularly
called the Metropolia, would pursue its own troubled course in the
Orthodox world.

The Detroit council gave the embattled Metropolia a clearer sense of
its institutional identity, but it could not prevent further divisions.

Although Kedrovsky's lawsuits met with little success on the parish level, he did win possession of the historic archdiocesan cathedral of St. Nicholas in New York City in 1925. In addition, two other groups entered into the struggle for the spiritual allegiance of Russian Orthodox Christians in America.

First on the scene was the Russian Orthodox Church Outside Russia, more often called the "Karlovtsy Synod" or simply "the Synod," which was organized in 1921 by a group of refugee Russian bishops in Sremski Karlovtsy, Yugoslavia. The Synod sought to unite all the scattered branches of the Russian Orthodox church outside the suffering Soviet Union. Metropolitan Platon initially cooperated with the Synod, but he quickly became disenchanted. He felt that the Synod exaggerated its claims to authority and that its political position, which favored Russia's old czarist regime, was out of date and embarrassing. Relations between the Metropolia and the Synod broke off in 1926, and the following year the Synod established its own rival diocese in America. A second period of cooperation, from 1935 to 1946, would flounder for essentially the same reasons.

Russian Orthodox bishops from outside the Soviet Union meet in Sremski Karlovtsy, Yugoslavia, in 1935. Among them, seated at the far left, is Metropolitan Theophilus of the North American Metropolia. Despite brief periods of cooperation, relations between these bishops were often tense, largely because of political differences.

The second competitor was the Russian patriarchal church itself. Following the death of Patriarch Tikhon in 1925, Metropolitan Sergius Stragorodsky, acting as a substitute in the role of patriarch, won a measure of recognition for the patriarchal church—at the price of a highly controversial declaration of loyalty to the Soviet state. Not surprisingly, Russian bishops outside the Soviet Union were reluctant to make any pledge, however vaguely worded, to refrain from anti-Soviet activity. In North America Metropolitan Platon was no exception. He refused to make the pledge, and the Metropolia reaffirmed its intention to remain a "temporarily self-governing church" with only "spiritual ties" to the suffering mother church in Russia. In response the Moscow patriarchate denounced the Metropolia as "schismatical," claiming that its actions created an illegitimate split in the church. In 1933 the Moscow patriarchate established its own jurisdiction in America.

Despite the establishment of these rival Russian jurisdictions, the vast majority of clergy and parishioners remained loyal to Metropolitan Platon and his successors, metropolitans Theophilus Pashkovsky (1934–50) and Leonty Turkevich (1950–65). Yet the struggles between these groups—and the positions they represented—left their mark on parish life, both for those who remained in the Metropolia and for those who left. After the Communist revolution, it became practically impossible for Orthodox Christians of Russian heritage in America not to be concerned with the fate of Russia and its church. Some insisted on the importance of loyalty to the mother church, the Moscow patriarchate, in spite of—or perhaps because of—its difficult circumstances in Soviet Russia. Others, believing that the patriarchal church had become a mere tool of the Soviet government, opposed that church to show their fidelity to the historic heritage of Russian Orthodoxy and their moral solidarity with the countless victims of Soviet oppression. People who held one or the other of these conflicting positions with particular zeal sometimes joined or formed a parish in the patriarchate or the Synod.

But many on both sides remained in the Metropolia, and their presence helps account for the wavering in Metropolia policy throughout this period. In general, those who remained loyal to the Metropolia valued its autonomy and its distinctive history in America above "Russian politics." Yet they could not escape the question of its relationship to other Russian groups. Emotions ran high in the Russian community in America. It was not uncommon for people to call those of different political views "Communists" or "monarchist fanatics." A bitter joke was repeated with many variations: A man was cast up on what appeared to be a desert island only to find that another person, a Russian, was already there. The man was given a quick tour of the island, and to his astonishment he was shown two churches. "Why," he asked the Russian, "are there two churches if you are the only person on this island?" The Russian explained, "This is the church I go to, and that is the church I *don't* go to."

As the leaders of the Russian archdiocese became absorbed in their own financial and administrative problems, they were no longer able or even particularly eager to maintain the multiethnic character of the archdiocese. As a result, the 1920s and 1930s saw the establishment of ethnically based "jurisdictions" that had ties to the various "mother churches" in Europe and the Middle East. The first of these in North America was the Greek Orthodox Archdiocese, which was established in 1921.

Greeks were among the most recent of the Orthodox "new immigrants" to arrive in America in large numbers. In 1900 there were only five Greek parishes scattered across the continent, but by 1918 there were about 140. These parishes had little contact with the Russian archdiocese, nor did they receive much supervision or pastoral care from any "mother church" overseas. A 1908 decree of the Patriarchate of Constantinople had placed them under the jurisdiction of the Church of Greece, but for a decade nothing was done to provide a bishop or organize church life. The Greek parishes remained in independent isolation. This situation changed in 1918 through the efforts of one of the most remarkable figures in 20th-century Orthodoxy, Meletios Metaxakis, who at the time was archbishop of Athens and head of the Church of Greece.

Meletios's activities came at a time of political turmoil in Greece. In 1917, as World War I was raging in Europe, Prime Minister Eleftherios

text continues on page 87

The Reminiscences of Father Constantine Vasilievich Popoff

Father Constantine Popoff, born and educated in Russia, first came to America as a young missionary priest in 1896.

Father Popoff served as the parish priest of St. Nicholas Russian Orthodox Greek Catholic Church in Joliet, Illinois, from 1931 to 1945, during the Great Depression. His reminiscences, written in 1962 on the parish's 55th anniversary, illustrate some of the financial and cultural challenges that ethnic parishes in America faced between World War I and World War II.

Arriving in Joliet, I took a taxi from the depot and told the driver to go to the Russian church. The taxi driver said, "In Joliet there are two Russian churches. One is small and the other is large. To which one do you want to go?" I answered that I didn't know, that I was here for the first time. The driver then said he would drive past the small church so I could see it. Later he would take me to the large one.

Soon we arrived at the small Russian church, stopped, and looked at the church. I saw on the steeple a three-barred cross, but, to make certain, I went to the church and read the sign, which was in English, "The Russian Orthodox Church of St. Nicholas." Then there was no doubt. I dismissed the taxi and with my baggage went to the door of the parish house, which was near the church. . . .

The secretary of the church committee, John Baloy, came. He acquainted me with the financial position of the church. The church didn't have any large debts but there were several bills which had remained unpaid, for example, for candles, coal, and the plumbing bills. . . . The secretary told me that unemployment had begun in the city last month. Two banks had stopped payment and closed, and many parishioners had lost their savings. . . .

The following Sunday I served divine liturgy in the Joliet church. Those in attendance numbered about 30 or 40, not including children. About a quarter of an hour before the services were to begin, Vasily Lucas came to me and said, "What should we do? We do not have any candles to sell to the parishioners." My answer was that I didn't know where it was possible to get candles on such short notice.

The elder then said, "I'm acquainted with the elder of the Serbian church, which is not far from us (about 5 minutes away). I will try to make a loan of a carton or two from him. We will return them later." I agreed with this idea. Soon he had brought one or two small boxes of candles before the service began.

I already knew that the parish did not have a reader or a choir director, but that there were several men who were able to read and to sing in church and some were able to lead the choir. I did not, however, expect to hear such wonderful women's voices. They were pleasant and strong. It was apparent that someone had taught them.

At the end of the service I said that Metropolitan Platon had appointed me rector of this parish, and I asked that the parish accept me as such. After the service the parishioners gathered at the church hall. I again repeated that which I had said in church, that I was the rector of the parish. Then they told me they were not able to pay a priest $105 a month as they had the former priest and that they were able to give only $75. I accepted that. One of the parishioners then asked me if there was going to be a parish school and, if so, when would it begin? I said that I could start tomorrow and that I had already suggested having school in the summertime from 9:00 in the morning to 12:00 noon and from 1:00 to 3:00 in the afternoon. In the wintertime, it could be from 4:00 to 6:00 in the evening and on Saturday mornings from 9:00 until 12:00 noon. . . .

Gradually there was only a small number of pupils who studied the Russian language (about 4 or 5 of them), so from 1940 on, the school was conducted in the English language. The children learned to sing in church at the liturgy and at vespers and at matins. On Saturdays the liturgy was studied and the children read and sang the parts which the reader was supposed to read.

But now to return to my other duties at the church. The elder at that time was Vasily Lucas, the treasurer, Max Kreche, the secretary, John Baloy. At the next

continued on next page

continued from previous page

committee meeting I asked the members where they had formerly bought candles and informed them it would be necessary to buy some now, at least 100 for $1.00. The committee agreed. And they suggested we send the order to Syracuse. I wrote to Syracuse about the candles. They answered that they would send the candles as soon as we paid the past bill, in the amount of $102.00. The candles were sent C.O.D., and it soon became necessary to send a check for $102.00 and afterwards to pay every time we received candles.

It was necessary to buy coal in the winter. This process repeated itself as with the candles. At the office where they sold coal they said we must pay the past bill; then they would send the coal. The total sum of this was about $20.00. So, we paid the bill and bought the church's coal. . . .

The parish numbered about 40 families, including bachelors, and only two had businesses. Many were without work and, if they did work, it was only about one or two days a week. It became necessary for the priest to visit the parishioners to collect the monthly dues, but very few paid their dues. There were about 15 or 20 who paid their dues every month, which was $1.00.

The parishioners of the church had taken all possible measures to better the material circumstances of the parish, and they did everything that was being done in other parishes. They organized church dinners, but there was only a small return from them, since their own people were few and it was difficult to bring in outsiders. . . . Picnics were held, and they often brought in a very small income, possibly $50. . . . The sisterhood organized parties for income to the church; one such party brought in more than $100. . . . We held plays, and all participants of these plays were our own parishioners. . . . All the plays were in the Russian language, except two that were played in English. The plays gave a small income, about $24.00 or $35.00. Once there were receipts of $50.00 when friends came from Chicago. . . .

When the European War [World War II] began, then the material circumstances of the parish changed greatly. I remember when the church income in 1932 was about $800, and in 1944 it became $1,600. The priest's salary in 1931 was $75.00 a month. In January of 1932, it was decreased to $60, and in January, 1933, it was decreased to $40.00. In October, 1937, it was increased to $50, and in 1939 it was increased to $60.00. In 1942 it was increased to $75.00.

text continued from page 83

Venizelos, a liberal who favored the British and French, forced the pro-German King Constantine into exile. Not long afterward Meletios, a supporter of Venizelos, became archbishop of Athens. Under his leadership the Church of Greece resolved at long last to organize the Greek parishes in America. Meletios himself traveled to America to oversee this project in 1918, and when he returned to Greece he appointed Bishop Alexander of Rodostolon as his resident representative in America, charged with bringing order and unity to the independent Greek parishes. This was not an easy task. Greeks in America were as divided over politics as their compatriots in Greece, with some supporting the king and others supporting Venizelos. Political strife inevitably affected church life on a local level. Some parishes, like St. Constantine in Brooklyn, were dominated by the royalists. Others were dominated by the Venizelists. When the parish of St. Eleftherios was formed in the Bronx in 1918, there was no question where its parishioners' loyalties lay—it was named for Venizelos's patron saint. Like the Russians, the Greeks during this period could point to "the church I go to" and "the church I *don't* go to."

Greek communities in America were divided in virtually every aspect of life. Theodore Saloutos, a pioneering historian of the Greek-American experience, recounts a comical episode from his childhood in Milwaukee, Wisconsin, in the 1920s. In those days Venizelists and royalists went to different churches. This division was echoed in the coffee houses that were the centers of social life for Greek-American men. "Each coffee house usually had a framed lithograph picture of its political idol suspended from the wall," Saloutos recalls, and "you patronized the coffee house of your political favorite and shunned that of his opponent." During the Christmas and New Year's seasons, Saloutos and a friend would go to these coffee houses to sing *kalanda,* or carols. This could become complicated, because the Greek churches—and therefore also the patrons of the coffee houses—were divided not only on political issues but also on which calendar they followed. The Venizelists used the "new calendar," which Meletios Metaxakis introduced in 1923, while the royalists continued to use the "old calendar." As a result, the Greek community of Milwaukee for some years celebrated two Christmases 13 days apart and two New Year's days, also 13 days apart. As Saloutos tells it, he and his friend "wanted to capitalize on the fact that the community was divided, because each time you sang the carols you received money from the host and others. So we decided to sing carols according to both the old and new calendar, which was not only non-partisan but more profitable." One day they made a mistake, however. What they believed was a royalist coffee house turned out to be a Venizelist stronghold. When Saloutos approached the proprietor of the coffee house about singing carols, the man picked up his cane and lunged at him, shouting, "You devil! Out! Out!"

Greek politics took a new turn in 1920. In elections that year, Venizelos was defeated, King Constantine returned from exile, and Archbishop Meletios Metaxakis was deposed. Still claiming to be the legitimate head of the Church of Greece, Meletios returned to the United States as an exile. Despite opposition from the now-royalist leaders of the Church of Greece, he and his colleague Bishop Alexander summoned the "First Clergy-Laity Congress" of Greek parishes in America. Meeting in New

Greek immigrants in Chicago enjoy each other's company as they prepare roast lamb over a charcoal fire.

York in September 1921, this historic assembly formally established the Greek Orthodox Archdiocese of North and South America. But before the end of the year, in another stunning development, Meletios, exiled archbishop of Athens, learned that he had been elected patriarch of Constantinople. In his enthronement speech in February 1922, Patriarch Meletios spoke eloquently of his vision for the future of Orthodoxy in America: "I saw the largest and the best of the Orthodox Church in the diaspora [that is, in regions where Orthodox Christians live dispersed from their native lands], and I understood how exalted the name of Orthodoxy could be, especially in the great country of the United States of America, if more than two million Orthodox people there were united into one church organization, an American Orthodox Church." The vision of a unified Orthodox church in America had returned.

Less than a month later, Meletios canceled the 1908 decree that had placed the Greek parishes in America under the jurisdiction of the Church of Greece. In May 1922 he issued a charter establishing the new American archdiocese as a part of the Patriarchate of Constantinople. The charter, however, was less sweeping in its vision of Orthodoxy in America than Meletios's enthronement speech had been. The archdiocese would have a distinctly Greek character. Its stated purpose was "to nurture the religious and moral life of American citizens of the Orthodox faith who are either themselves Greek or of Greek ancestry."

Bishop Alexander was appointed as head of the new American archdiocese, but unfortunately he could not end the strife between royalists and Venizelists. In 1921 the Church of Greece sent its own representative, who organized about 50 largely royalist parishes in opposition to Alexander. He was recalled in 1923, but another rival bishop, Metropolitan Vasilios Komvopoulos, appeared on the scene later the same year and organized a group of royalist parishes as the "Autocephalous Greek Orthodox Church of the United States and Canada." Only in 1930 did a measure of order return. Recognizing the need for cooperation, the Patriarchate of Constantinople and the Church of Greece recalled all the feuding bishops from America and appointed a new archbishop, the dynamic young metropolitan of Corfu, Athenagoras Spirou.

Greek Orthodox women decorate their church in preparation for Holy Saturday services, during which Christ's burial will be commemorated. Soon, on Easter Sunday, the flowers adorning this "tomb" will be rearranged to honor Christ's resurrection.

Although Athenagoras came to America with the reputation of being a Venizelist, he insisted from the start that "the church is to become the mother of everyone and to love and understand people irrespective of their political affiliations." Soon after his arrival in February 1931, he made an exhausting series of parish visits aimed at ending political strife and promoting loyalty to the Patriarchate of Constantinople. He also introduced a new archdiocesan charter that centralized administration and curbed the power of parish boards of trustees, especially in assigning and dismissing clergy. Despite a series of lawsuits by those who regarded Athenagoras as a "dictator," his personal charm won him overwhelming support within the archdiocese. As one parishioner remarked, "Even his official letters sounded as though they were addressed personally to each one of us."

In 1948 Athenagoras's tenure in America came to an end with his election as patriarch of Constantinople. By that time, the Greek Orthodox Archdiocese had become the largest and most influential Orthodox jurisdiction in America. It could boast a theological seminary (first in Pomfret, Connecticut, then in Brookline, Massachusetts), an orphanage (in Garrison, New York), an archdiocesan newspaper, and an exceptionally active national women's organization known as the Philoptochos ("Friends of the Poor"). The number of parishes had tripled to more than 400, most with Greek schools and cultural centers attached. The archdiocesan budget had increased from $22,000 in 1932 to more than $100,000 in 1948. The archdiocese—and its archbishop—had become a significant presence in American public life. When Athenagoras had first come to the United States in 1931, few had turned out to meet him, and only the Greek-American press covered the event. But when he left for his enthronement as patriarch of Constantinople, thousands watched him board President Truman's private plane for the trip to Istanbul, and his photo appeared on the cover of *Life* magazine.

The Greek archdiocese was but the first of many Orthodox jurisdictions to be formed along ethnic lines in America during the 1920s and 1930s. Virtually all these jurisdictions still exist today, and they continue to mold the way in which their parishioners understand and experience Orthodox church life. Like the Russian and Greek jurisdictions, they have their own unique and sometimes complex histories, their own heroes, and their own historic sites, just as they have their own foods and folk dances and often their own distinctive languages.

Most of the early Serbian Orthodox parishes in America had belonged to the multiethnic Russian archdiocese, but in 1921, in the wake of the Communist revolution in Russia, they were chartered as a diocese by the Serbian patriarchate in Belgrade. Their first administrator was Bishop Nikolai Velimirovich, one of the most noted spiritual leaders of the modern Serbian church and widely venerated as a saint. The actual work of organizing the diocese, however, fell to his assistant, Father Mardarije Uskokovich, who earlier had administered the Serbian parishes when they formed part of the Russian archdiocese. In 1927 Mardarije became the first resident bishop of the new Serbian diocese. His many accomplishments include establishment of St. Sava's Monastery near Libertyville, Illinois, where his grave is a place of pilgrimage for Serbian Orthodox Christians in America to this day.

Albanian Orthodox parishes, headed by Father Theophan Noli, also had formed part of the Russian archdiocese. Noli was an ardent nationalist who would eventually translate not only the services of the Orthodox church but also the works of Shakespeare, Cervantes, and many other literary giants into the Albanian language. He had begun organizing the church and community life of Albanian immigrants as early as 1908, and in 1919 the Russian archdiocese had elected him as a bishop. Confirmation from Russia never came, however. When he eventually was

This shop in Chicago's "Greek Town" announces itself as the "Phoenix Greek Bakery," specializing in Greek pastries and other Greek products. As the icon and fancy cakes in the window suggest, Easter is at hand.

ordained, it was in Albania, as head of an independent Albanian church. For a time Archbishop Theophan even served as prime minister of Albania, but after being forced into exile he eventually returned to the United States, where he established the Albanian Orthodox Archdiocese in America in 1932.

The situation of the Syrio-Arab Orthodox parishes was more complex. In the days of Bishop Raphael Hawaweeny, the Arabs within the

Russian archdiocese had been the most visible sign that the Orthodox in America could achieve structural unity without the loss of ethnic identity. But in the 1920s the struggle in the Arab community intensified between "Antacky," or pro-Antiochians, and "Russy," or pro-Russians. In 1924 a number of parishes were accepted into the jurisdiction of the Patriarchate of Antioch through the work of Bishop Victor Abu-Assaly. Others remained loyal to Bishop Aftimios Ofiesh, an impractical idealist who earlier had headed the Syrio-Arab subdivision of the Russian archdiocese but now headed an independent "American Orthodox Catholic church." In 1934 Bishop Victor died, and in the same year Bishop Aftimios married and resigned as bishop. Their departure, however, did not end the split within the Arab Orthodox community. On the very same day in 1936,

rival bishops were ordained in New York and Toledo. The energetic Archbishop Antony Bashir in New York quickly won the allegiance of the vast majority of Antiochian parishes. Under his leadership, the Antiochian Orthodox Christian Archdiocese became one of the best-organized and most efficient Orthodox jurisdictions in America. But his rival in Toledo, Bishop Samuel David, also was eventually recognized by the Patriarchate of Antioch. As a result, two Antiochian jurisdictions existed side by side in America until 1975.

Bulgarian Orthodox immigrants began to arrive in North America in small numbers in the early 1900s. Spread thinly across the continent, they usually attended Russian Orthodox churches, but beginning in 1907 they formed a few independent parishes. The Bulgarian Orthodox church in Sofia began efforts to organize these scattered parishes in 1922, but did not send a resident bishop until 1938.

Organization of church life among Romanian Orthodox immigrants presented an unusual constellation of problems. Like the Greeks, the Romanians were highly transient. More than two-thirds of those who came to the United States before World War I returned to Romania when

Archbishop Theophan (Fan) Noli founded the Albanian Orthodox Archdiocese in America. Archbishop Theophan is famous for his many translations into the Albanian language, but he also produced eight volumes of liturgical texts and music in English, so that young Albanian-Americans could participate more fully in the church's worship.

Bishop Polycarp Morusca (left) arrives on a pastoral visit. He is being welcomed with bread and salt, a traditional symbol of hospitality in Eastern Europe.

the borders of their homeland were extended after the war. Those who remained in North America were, like the Arabs and Bulgarians, widely dispersed. And because they spoke a Romance language closely related to French and Italian, they did not fit in well in the churches of their Russian and other Slavic neighbors, all of whom spoke Slavic languages. As early as 1902 in Canada and 1904 in the United States, the Romanians formed independent parishes served by priests from Europe. Not until 1929, in Detroit, did the Romanian parishes of North America hold their first congress. The congress asked the Romanian church to establish a North American diocese under its jurisdiction but with considerable autonomy. Six years later the new diocese's first bishop arrived. He was the capable and energetic Polycarp Morusca, who in a brief but productive pastorate founded a weekly diocesan newspaper, organized youth and women's groups, and established the "Vatra Romanesca"—the "Romanian home"—as a spiritual center for his far-flung diocese. Located in Grass Lake, Michigan, the Vatra complex houses a small monastic community as well as the diocesan administration.

Most immigrant groups found it fairly easy to form a relationship with a well-established "mother church" in the Old World. For a few, however, political circumstances made this difficult. Such was the case with the Ukrainians, whose homeland had been part of the Russian Empire and was to become part of the Soviet Union. In the early 20th century the growing sense of national identity among Ukrainians in the United States led them to form the Ukrainian National Church, which by design was altogether independent of the Russian archdiocese and all other Orthodox churches. Similar impulses in Canada led to the formation of a very large independent jurisdiction there. Both groups, however, faced the same difficulty: the lack of bishops.

When the Russian Empire broke up after the Communist revolution, a short-lived Ukrainian National Republic was established, and with it, a self-proclaimed Ukrainian Autocephalous Orthodox Church. None of the other Orthodox churches recognized the Ukrainian church because of irregularities in the ordination of its first bishops, but both the Ukrainian Orthodox Church of the U.S.A. and the Ukrainian Orthodox Church of Canada welcomed its establishment and petitioned it for a bishop. In 1924 Archbishop John Theodorovich arrived from Ukraine to head both churches. Unfortunately, because of the circumstances surrounding their establishment, these two Ukrainian jurisdictions were regarded as uncanonical, or illegitimate, by the other Orthodox jurisdictions in America. For decades they were largely cut off from wider Orthodox church life. They established relations with the other Eastern Orthodox churches only when they were received into the jurisdiction of the Patriarchate of Constantinople in 1990 (for the Canadian church) and 1995 (for the church in the United States).

In the 1930s, two other groups also faced the problem of establishing a diocesan structure under a bishop's authority in the absence of a well-established "mother church" in the Old World. These groups consisted of Eastern Catholics, or Uniates—those whose formerly Orthodox churches had been absorbed into the Catholic church. But when the pope in 1929 decreed that all newly ordained and newly arrived Eastern Catholic priests serving in America must be celibate, or unmarried, many Eastern Catholic Ukrainians and Carpatho-Russians in America strongly objected. They wanted to retain the Orthodox tradition that allowed married priests, so they left the Eastern Catholic church in a second "return of the Unia" to Orthodoxy. But to whom should these Eastern Catholics turn? To the Russian church, following the path of Father Alexis Toth in the previous century? They were not ethnic Russians and did not want to be "russified." There was an alternative. The Patriarchate of Constantinople claimed that the ancient church laws gave it exclusive authority over the "diaspora," that is, over Orthodox Christians in regions outside the limits of the other autocephalous Orthodox churches. As a result, a group of former Ukrainian Eastern Catholics entered the jurisdiction of the patriarch of Constantinople in 1937 as the Ukrainian Orthodox Church in America. The following year a large group of Carpatho-Russians followed a similar course, forming the American Carpatho-Russian Orthodox Greek Catholic Diocese of the U.S.A.

By the late 1930s, a new structure for Orthodoxy in America had emerged. It was unlike anything Archbishop Evdokim could have imagined when he submitted his 1916 report to the Russian Holy Synod. Instead of one American Orthodox church moving under Russian guidance toward full ecclesiastical independence, there were more than a dozen ethnic churches linked to nearly as many "mother churches" in Europe and the Middle East. While this new structure had some disadvantages, it was practically inevitable in view of the chaos that all the Orthodox immigrant groups in America faced in the 1920s. Indeed, many people must have felt that the ethnic jurisdiction was the natural and obvious way for American Orthodoxy to be organized. The ethnic structure gave groups that otherwise might have been submerged in the maelstrom of American society a way to preserve and celebrate their distinctive identities as well as their Orthodox faith.

A number of forces seemed to threaten these distinctive ethnic identities, particularly during the 1920s. Among other things, restrictive federal legislation reduced new immigration to a trickle. For example, the provisions of the National Origins Quota Act of 1924 limited Greek immigration to 100 persons per year. In contrast, 28,000 Greek immigrants had entered the United States in 1921, the last year of relatively open immigration. During the days of open immigration, relatively few of those who came to America expected to stay for the rest of their lives. Their ethnic and religious identities were secure. They were Greeks—or Russians or Romanians—who happened to be living and working in America for a time. But after the closing of immigration, this changed. Whether or not they meant to do so, many ethnic Americans "lost" various aspects of their identities. For example, they adopted new American-sounding names so that it would be easier for them to blend into American life—Vladimir might become Walter, and Anagnostopoulos might become Agnew. They married outside their own group and encouraged their children to speak only English, because they were Americans now. And along the way, many of them left the Orthodox church.

But some resisted the pressure to assimilate, or join the mainstream. For these people, the ethnic church and church-related ethnic organizations offered a variety of ways to maintain links with their heritage. The Greek school, the Russian school, or the Ukrainian school, meeting for several hours after "American school" and on Saturdays, taught the rudiments of ethnic language and history to children who might otherwise have been enjoying a game of baseball with their non-Greek, non-Russian,

The first convention of the Federated Russian Orthodox Clubs (FROC) met in Pittsburgh in 1927. Organizations like FROC gave "hyphenated Americans," such as Greek-Americans and Russian-Americans, a sense of pride in their Old World heritage.

or non-Ukrainian peers. In the process, these children learned how special their own nation's language and culture was. Organizations like the Federated Russian Orthodox Clubs (FROC) and the Serbian Singing Federation (SSF) organized social and cultural activities ranging from speech contests to basketball tournaments on local, regional, and national levels. Church leaders such as Archbishop Athenagoras were spokesmen for ethnic causes and symbols of ethnic dignity. But above all, the church services themselves reminded ethnic Orthodox Christians of their Old World identity. Seemingly unchanged and unchangeable even in their language and musical style, the solemnities of the liturgy were a welcome element of continuity and stability in an ever-changing New World.

Although the system of ethnic jurisdictions helped many Orthodox Christians in America to preserve their Orthodox identity, it did so at a price. Divided and separated, the various jurisdictions lacked the financial and human resources to support the full range of social service and educational programs that had served Orthodox Christians in America before the Communist revolution in Russia. For example, the theological seminary that Archbishop Tikhon had founded in 1905 closed its doors in 1923 for lack of funds. More serious was the fact that the ethnic structure tended to obscure certain basic aspects of Orthodox Christianity itself. The ethnic jurisdictions often formed closed groups, cut off from the wider American context. A parish therefore might not welcome new members, particularly if they were of a different ethnic background. Concern for mission, for bringing the message of Orthodoxy to new cultural contexts, was lost. In addition, the system of ethnic jurisdictions seriously distorted the traditional Orthodox understanding of church order. According to Orthodox theology, the church is supposed to be structured in a way that unites all the faithful in a given place, regardless of their ethnic and linguistic differences—in 1872, in fact, a church council in Constantinople had condemned organization along purely ethnic lines as a form of heresy, or violation of church doctrine. The existence of parallel ethnic jurisdictions, something unknown in traditional Old World Orthodoxy, gravely compromised Orthodoxy's message of unity in Christ.

During this period, most active church leaders took it for granted that preserving the Orthodox faith in America depended on preserving ethnic identity, especially language. But a few lonely individuals questioned this assumption. For example, in the early 1920s Bishop Joachim Alexopoulos in the Greek Orthodox Archdiocese argued that English-language Sunday schools would be more effective than Greek schools for "moulding character and preserving religious and ethnic values." English, he predicted, would inevitably replace Greek as the living language of the faithful in America. If the wider cultural values important to Orthodoxy were to survive, young people must be given a deeper understanding of the Orthodox faith itself, apart from language instruction.

More influential than Bishop Joachim was Metropolitan Antony Bashir of the Antiochian Orthodox Archdiocese, who took the lead in encouraging the use of English, developing Sunday school programs, and welcoming American converts into his jurisdiction. Reflecting in 1957 on his decades of pastoral work in America, he said: "While we must still minister to many who remember the ways and customs of another land, it is our policy to make the Church in the United States an American Church. . . . From the beginning of my ministry, I began printing English service books and training English-speaking priests. We are tied to no sacred language; we recognize all tongues as the creation of God and employ them in our worship. We have no desire to perpetuate anything but the Gospel of Christ, and that we can do as effectively in English as in any other tongue."

A few went so far as to single out the ethnic jurisdiction itself as the greatest obstacle to the healthy development of Orthodoxy in America. In 1927 the idealistic Bishop Aftimios Ofiesh published a remarkable article entitled "The Present and Future of Orthodoxy in America." As a result of the jurisdictional system, he argued, Orthodoxy "is Herself in America the most outstanding horrible example of the disastrous effects of disunion, disorder, secret strife, and open warfare that this country of divided and warring sects can offer." Following World War I, "each little group of Orthodox produced some new party or leader who wished to set up in America a Church based solely on the national or racial derivation of its adherents. The inclusive unity and coordination of Orthodoxy as such in America regardless of nationality or language was forgotten in this sudden over-emphasis upon political or tribal distinctions.... The true ideal of one Orthodox Catholic Church in America for the growing thousands of Americans born and reared in Orthodoxy was lost in the over-zealous patriotic desire of the immigrant generation to parallel in America the national resurrections taking place in Europe." How could this situation be corrected? According to Bishop Aftimios, the only feasible solution was "the formation of an American Synod of United Orthodoxy," independent of the national churches of Europe and the Middle East.

Bishop Aftimios's strong words found scarcely an echo in his own day. The "American Orthodox Catholic Church" he attempted to establish won few followers and lasted only a few years. But although most Orthodox church leaders seem to have been untroubled by the existence of parallel ethnic jurisdictions, some of them were keenly aware of the need for closer cooperation between these jurisdictions. In 1934 Archbishop Athenagoras of the Greek Orthodox Archdiocese proposed the establishment of a theological seminary that would serve the needs of all the Orthodox jurisdictions in America. In 1937 he and Metropolitan Antony Bashir of the Antiochian Orthodox Archdiocese suggested a conference of Orthodox bishops that would bring together the heads of the various jurisdictions. Unfortunately, Metropolitan Theophilus of the Metropolia, the second-largest Orthodox jurisdiction in America, turned down both of these proposals. At the time he was more concerned about preserving his church's Russian heritage.

Only slightly more successful was another project of Archbishop Athenagoras and Metropolitan Antony: the establishment in 1943 of an organization called the Federated Orthodox Greek Catholic Primary Jurisdictions in America. During the two years of its existence the federation succeeded in gaining for Orthodox clergy the same draft-exempt military status that Catholic, Protestant, and Jewish clergy enjoyed, but it did not significantly improve Orthodox unity in America. At the insistence of the resident bishop of the Moscow patriarchate, membership in the federation was limited to jurisdictions with a direct association with a mother church in the Old World. This excluded the large Metropolia.

As these feeble efforts at cooperation between jurisdictions suggest, Orthodox Christians in America in the mid-1900s were divided not only by languages and customs, but also by Old World politics. As a result, their church lacked the kind of structural unity that Orthodox theology itself demands. After the 1940s many of these people would discover a common sense of Orthodox identity that went beyond ethnic differences. Their calls for Orthodox unity in America would become more insistent. But they would also discover that the question of Orthodox unity in America remained closely linked to political developments affecting Orthodoxy elsewhere in the world.

Chapter 5

The Quest for Unity

Since the mid-20th century the ethnic jurisdiction has remained one of the most visible features of Orthodoxy in America. When Orthodoxy is mentioned, people tend to think first of its ethnic aspect. Orthodox Christians who are asked about their religious affiliation almost always add an ethnic qualifier—Greek, Serbian, Russian, Ukrainian, or the like. In the decades immediately following World War II (1939–45), the number of such jurisdictions in America increased, mostly because of political changes in Eastern Europe. Some of the new jurisdictions were formed by smaller ethnic groups—such as the Belorusians or Estonians—that had not been represented earlier. Others resulted from political divisions within ethnic groups.

But even as the number of jurisdictions multiplied, Orthodoxy in America was changing from within. The socially mobile, English-speaking, American-educated children and grandchildren of the immigrants, as well as the many Americans who had converted to Orthodoxy, were not particularly interested in European cultural differences and politics. They were less inclined than their parents to regard religious faith and ethnic identity as inseparable. From the 1960s onward, they helped create a powerful impulse toward Orthodox unity in America.

World War II brought sweeping political changes in Eastern Europe that had important consequences for the Orthodox churches there. In the

Soviet Union, the church had helped rally the Russian people in support of the war effort, and Soviet leader Joseph Stalin returned the favor by ending government efforts to exterminate the faith. Churches reopened for worship. New patriarchal elections were held. The Russian Orthodox church was even encouraged to assume a position of leadership in the Orthodox world. But all this came at a price. The government strictly limited and closely supervised all church activities, and it regularly harassed believers, particularly if they called for greater freedom for the church. Soon after the war, as Soviet-style Communist governments were set up throughout Eastern Europe, much the same pattern for church life was imposed on the Orthodox churches that came under their authority. Although these churches were allowed to function, they could hardly do so freely.

These changes in Eastern Europe affected Orthodox church life in America. Now Romanians, Bulgarians, Serbs, and Albanians, their numbers increased by political refugees and displaced persons fleeing from the Communist takeover in Eastern Europe, had to face the kinds of issues that Russians in America had faced after the Communist revolution of 1917. Some emphasized the importance of remaining faithful to the mother church. They pointed out that the present situation, while difficult, was considerably better than the situation in Russia in the 1920s, when the Soviet government had aimed at the total elimination of the church. Even under the new Communist political system, they argued, the church could still carry out its essential tasks.

Other people, however, maintained that the church and its leaders were being unacceptably manipulated by the Communist state, to the point that the integrity and freedom even of the church's American diocese were in danger. They asked: How can we trust a bishop whose appointment depends on the approval of the Communist authorities? How can we speak out freely about religious oppression in the homeland if we remain ecclesiastically dependent on the mother church? Such debates divided families, split parishes, and shattered the moral and institutional solidarity of ethnic jurisdictions as hostile factions battled in the courts for control of church property. Typically, a militantly anti-Communist group would form an independent, "free" jurisdiction, and those loyal to the mother church would denounce this jurisdiction as "uncanonical" and "schismatic" (illegal and unauthorized). At one point or another during the cold war period, from the late 1940s into the 1980s, the Romanians, Bulgarians, Serbs, and Albanians in America all experienced something with which the Russians were already familiar: In almost every major population center they could point to "the church I go to" and "the church I *don't* go to."

During this period, the institutional structure of Orthodoxy in America became more fragmented than ever. At the same time, however, individual Orthodox Christians were beginning to discover a common Orthodox identity. They were not ashamed of their immigrant background and ethnic heritage, but if asked about their religious affiliation, they might answer simply that they were Orthodox or, if pushed to add a qualifier, describe themselves as American Orthodox.

Changing patterns of immigration contributed to this new sense of identity. Massive immigration of Orthodox Christians ended in the 1920s. The arrival of Eastern European refugees after World War II did bring the tensions of the cold war to some communities, but it did not significantly alter the composition of most parishes. A steadily increasing percentage of church members had been born and educated in the United States. Many had proven their patriotism by serving in the U.S. armed forces in World War II and the Korean War, and they had returned with new confidence. They were proud to be American, and they were proud to be Orthodox. Many moved to the suburbs, physically and psychologically miles away from the ethnic neighborhoods of their youth. But even those who did not move differed from the Orthodox Christians of their parents' and grandparents' generations. They were less afraid of new things. They wanted more use of English in church, so that their spouses, often from non-Orthodox backgrounds, would feel more comfortable. They wanted religious education for their children and for themselves. They campaigned

The Birth of a Pan-Orthodox Mission Parish

Annette Milkovich and her husband Zoran were among the founding members of St. Anthony's Orthodox Church in suburban Bergenfield, New Jersey. In many ways, St. Anthony's was typical of the pan-ethnic "mission parishes" established in the decades following World War II. Mrs. Milkovich's account of its first years gives a good picture of the novelty and excitement that the founders of these parishes experienced.

"To establish a multiethnic parish in Bergen County, N.J., and to adopt English for use in the services" was the goal of seven Arab-American Orthodox families when they asked the late Metropolitan Antony Bashir for his archpastoral blessing in April 1956. With permission granted, the founders advertised their intentions in the major county newspaper and obtained the use of a small chapel of St. Paul's Episcopal Church in Englewood.

Initially we had no priest, so a reader led the little congregation in the Typica [a prayer service of psalms and readings] on Sunday mornings. Throughout that spring and summer, families of Arab, Greek, Russian, Serbian, and Ukrainian backgrounds living in the surrounding suburban towns began to attend services. Soon a multiethnic Church Development Committee was formed.

After Labor Day of 1956, with the permission of Metropolitan Antony and cooperation of Metropolitan Leonty of the Metropolia, the committee asked Father Joseph Kreta, from the Metropolia's cathedral in New York City, to serve the first Divine Liturgy [the eucharistic service of the Orthodox church]. The celebration of that liturgy in a well-filled chapel was proof that this new type of parish could succeed. First, however, a permanent priest was needed. For a few months priests from several jurisdictions served on a temporary basis. Then, in January 1957, Zoran Milkovich, a member of the committee, received a phone call from a Russian priest without a parish, Father Stephen Lishevsky. He said that although his conversational English was poor, he could serve the Divine Liturgy in English.

He was hardly the "young American priest" that the committee had envisioned, but they had no choice. Father Lishevsky came each Sunday for many months. His liturgical English was good, and his piety soon overcame any initial objections. Nevertheless, it was fortunate that after a

A conference of Orthodox People Together (OPT), a lay-led group formed in the 1980s to promote Orthodox cooperation and unity in America. Groups like OPT reflect the pan-Orthodox spirit that earlier led to the formation of parishes like St. Anthony's.

few months an Arab-American student at St. Vladimir's Seminary, Gabriel Ashie, came to assist and to give the sermons.

The new community soon was too large for the little chapel at St. Paul's, so for several years we rented a Masonic temple in Englewood. This gave us more room for services and for a coffee hour afterward, and we also were able to begin a Sunday school program. But this also meant that each week we had to set up a temporary church, with icons and candlestands and other items borrowed from many sources. Everyone had to pitch in. Our makeshift church was not as magnificent as the churches that most of us had attended previously, but we did feel wonderfully close to God and to each other.

In 1958 Gabriel Ashie was ordained a priest and assigned to the new parish by Metropolitan Antony. Within a few years a beautiful church was built in Bergenfield, bordering on Englewood and Tenafly. Pimen Sofronov, the most famous iconographer in this hemisphere, painted the icons for the iconostasis. By that point, the congregation was more than 100 families—30 percent Slavs, 30 percent Arabs, 30 percent Greeks, and 10 percent converts. The phenomenon of the pan-ethnic parish in suburban New Jersey was realized!

for the introduction of the "new calendar" in jurisdictions that did not already use it.

In time this new generation would leave its mark on the older ethnic parishes, but its earliest and most distinctive contribution to Orthodoxy in America was the formation of new mission parishes, first in the suburbs, then in regions such as the Sun Belt states of the West and South where the population was growing rapidly. Parishes like St. Innocent's in suburban Los Angeles (1954), St. Anthony's in suburban New Jersey (1956), and scores of later imitators gave Orthodoxy a new and distinctly American face. Most of these parishes were deliberately inclusive, open to members of all ethnic groups, and thought of themselves as part of a larger Orthodox community. Most used English for worship, though from time to time they might add snatches of Greek, Church Slavonic, Romanian, or Arabic to make everyone feel at home. They drew on a variety of Orthodox musical traditions. They promoted theological education and liturgical renewal. They took pride in establishing a strong sense of community without the support of a common ethnic background. A coffee hour following the Sunday morning Divine Liturgy became a standard feature of parish life.

The distinctive religious style of these new parishes reflected important developments in Orthodox theology and theological education in America. No Orthodox theological seminary had functioned in America from 1923 until the late 1930s, when Holy Cross Greek Orthodox School of Theology (1937, first located in Pomfret, Connecticut, later in Brookline, Massachusetts) and St. Vladimir's Orthodox Theological Seminary (1938, first located in New York City, later in Crestwood, New York) were founded. After World War II these new schools began to make an impact on Orthodox church life. American Orthodox Christians could now study theology in their own country. Their teachers included a number of internationally renowned theologians who came to the United States after the war. Seminarians heard Father Georges Florovsky lecture on the theology of the early fathers of the church, which he contrasted with the dry textbook theology of more recent times. They heard Father

Alexander Schmemann lecture on "liturgical theology" and draw attention to the importance of the Eucharist for community life: The church, he insisted, expresses its faith most completely when its members gather together in worship and receive Holy Communion, becoming one body with Christ and with one another. After decades of isolation, America had entered into the vanguard of 20th-century Orthodox theology.

This theological revival had a particularly powerful effect on the life of the new parishes formed in the postwar years. Typically the founders of these parishes would ask their bishop for a young American priest. They usually received one—older priests with distinguished records of service generally went to well-established ethnic parishes, not to struggling new missions. In their new parishes, these young priests, often recent graduates of Holy Cross or

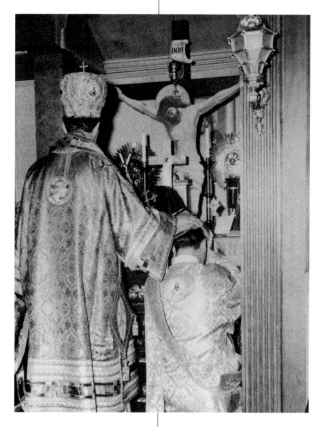

St. Vladimir's, tried to put into practice what they had learned at seminary. For example, they developed comprehensive programs of parish education that included not only Sunday schools for children but also Bible study groups and lecture series for adults. Orthodox church members in America had participated in church decision-making and parish management for a long time, particularly when finances were involved. In the past this sometimes had resulted in conflicts between parish lay leaders and their priest: Lay leaders tended to regard the priest's role as purely "spiritual," limited to performance of the church services, and to view with suspicion any attempt on his part to become involved in the "material" aspects of the parish's life. Now, with a deeper understanding of the church as a worshiping community united as the one body of Christ, lay leaders were better able to appreciate the need for cooperation in all

On the Sunday of the Veneration of the Holy Cross, a young deacon is ordained to the priesthood in the chapel of Holy Cross Greek Orthodox School of Theology in Brookline, Massachusetts. Since 1937, Holy Cross has trained young men and women for service in the Greek Orthodox Archdiocese, now the largest of the Orthodox jurisdictions in America.

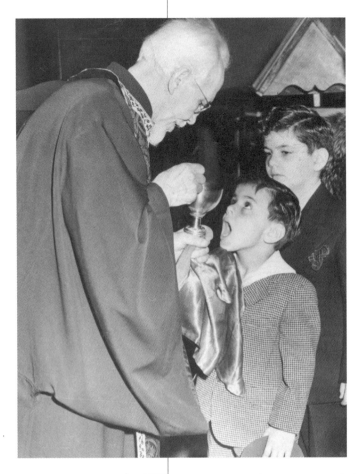

Since World War II, regular reception of holy communion has become a noteworthy feature of parish life in many Orthodox parishes in America.

aspects of parish life. In time, a theologically informed membership would become one of the distinguishing features of Orthodoxy in America.

Influenced especially by the example of Father Schmemann, these young priests also introduced a number of liturgical reforms that, though they struck some "old-timers" as innovations, were based on the practices of the early church. For example, during the church services priests began saying important prayers aloud rather than reciting them silently. They introduced a fuller cycle of liturgical services, particularly during Lent and Holy Week, than most of their parishioners had been accustomed to. They encouraged frequent and regular communion during the Eucharist (for centuries Orthodox worshippers had tended to receive communion only three or four times a year). Through such efforts they restored worship to a central place in the life of the church community.

Not everyone was enthusiastic about the changes encouraged by the new parishes and their young priests. The extensive use of English in church services proved particularly controversial in many jurisdictions. Under the leadership of Metropolitan Antony Bashir (1936–66) and his successor Metropolitan Philip Saliba (1966–), the Antiochian Orthodox Archdiocese was the first jurisdiction to institute the widespread use of English. The Metropolia followed, very slowly in the 1950s, more rapidly in the 1960s and 1970s. But the use of English met with greater resistance in jurisdictions with a strong ethnic consciousness—for example, the Ukrainian church in Canada rejected the use of English for church services as late as the 1980s.

Nowhere was debate about language livelier than in the Greek Ortho-dox Archdiocese. On the one hand, most Greek Orthodox Americans were as fully integrated into American life as their counterparts in the Antiochian Orthodox Archdiocese and the Metropolia. They used English in religious education and in administration. They had begun to use English for some prayers, the creed, and scripture readings during church services. In 1970 Archbishop Iakovos Coucouzes, head of the archdiocese (1958–96), courageously proposed even wider use of English, in view of "the two present American-born generations, mixed marriages, the indigenization of our Church, the educational level of our children, the limited Greek preparation of our priests." His proposal met with vigorous opposition on the part of a small but vocal minority. A group devoted to "preservation of the Greek language and the Greek Orthodox Church" was organized, and it called for the archbishop's removal. Eventually the storm subsided. Patriarch Athenagoras of Constantinople declared that "the Greek language is and will remain the basic and preeminent liturgical language of the Greek Orthodox Archdiocese of America." Athenagoras's carefully chosen words did not mean that parishes could not use English in worship, and after 1970 the use of English would steadily increase within the archdiocese. But the incident showed how sensitive the language issue remained in the Greek Ortho-dox world.

Slowly, but seemingly inevitably, Orthodoxy entered into the mainstream of religious and public life in America in the 1950s and 1960s. The major jurisdictions participated in the work of ecumenical bodies such as the National Council of Churches of Christ (NCCC) and the World Council of Churches (WCC). Orthodox priests became chaplains in the U.S. armed forces. Church leaders gained greater visibility on the nation's stage. In 1957, for example, Archbishop Michael Constantinides, head of the Greek Orthodox Archdiocese (1949–58), became the first Orthodox bishop to take part in a presidential inauguration. In 1967 his successor, Archbishop Iakovos, made headlines when he walked with Martin Luther King, Jr., and other civil rights leaders in the march on Selma, Alabama.

Most Orthodox Christians in America rejoiced at these developments.

They were optimistic even when controversies erupted over issues such as language and liturgical reform, viewing such controversies as signs that their church was taking seriously the challenge of adjusting to American life and needs. Many also were optimistic about the prospects for greater Orthodox unity in America. As the various Orthodox jurisdictions became less preoccupied with ethnic issues and more involved in American life, sociological obstacles to unity were breaking down. And as people rediscovered their common ancient traditions of worship and spirituality, theological reasons for unity were becoming more compelling.

The spirit of optimism of the 1950s and 1960s expressed itself in several cooperative programs and agencies that spanned jurisdictions. On a local level, Orthodox clergy formed associations. On college campuses, Orthodox Christian Fellowships (OCFs) sprang up, bringing together students from across jurisdictional lines to hear lectures by notable speakers like Florovsky and Schmemann and experience the novelty of worship in English. On the national level, Orthodox Christians involved in the Boy Scouts and Girl Scouts of America formed a commission on scouting. But perhaps the most significant development was the establishment of an Orthodox Christian Education Commission in 1956. During the preceding decade, virtually all the Orthodox jurisdictions in America had established Sunday schools and other educational programs for their children. The materials produced for these programs varied in quality and represented a wasteful duplication of

Archbishop Iakovos Coucouzes (left) joins Reverend Martin Luther King, Jr., at the march for civil rights in Selma, Alabama.

effort. Mrs. Sophie Koulomzin was determined to do something about this regrettable situation. Born in Russia in 1903, Koulomzin had fled after the Communist revolution. In France she began her pioneering work in Orthodox Christian education. Later she moved to the United States with her husband and four children and began organizing religious education conferences that eventually brought together representatives from most of the Orthodox jurisdictions in America. The resulting Orthodox Christian Education Commission (OCEC) showed that successful Orthodox collaboration on a national level was both possible and desirable. (In the 1980s, as communism loosened its grip on her native land, Koulomzin—by this point a great-grandmother—would turn her boundless energy to producing religious education materials for Russia.)

A new phase in the quest for Orthodox unity in America began in 1960, with the creation of the Standing Conference of Canonical Orthodox Bishops in the Americas (SCOBA). Soon after his arrival in the United States, Archbishop Iakovos, new head of the Greek Orthodox Archdiocese, proposed a conference of bishops that would bring together the heads of the various jurisdictions for consultation and common action. Most of the jurisdictions accepted his proposal. The most significant exceptions were the Russian Orthodox Church Outside Russia and the Ukrainian Orthodox Church of the U.S.A., both of which declined to participate because the Moscow patriarchal jurisdiction was involved. Despite their absence, the first SCOBA conference was the most representative and comprehensive gathering of Orthodox bishops that had yet occurred in America. Under the leadership of Archbishop Iakovos, it would bring a previously unheard-of degree of unity to Orthodoxy in America.

During the first decade of its existence, SCOBA became an important agency for cooperation between the Orthodox jurisdictions in America. It took under its wing the OCEC and the Orthodox Scouting Commission and supported the establishment of various other organizations to oversee grassroots activities. These included a Commission on Military Chaplaincies; an Ecumenical Commission to establish policies on relations

In this Sunday school in Alaska, an Orthodox nun helps children and parents prepare icon prints for mounting.

with other Christian groups and supervise dialogue with them; and a Campus Commission to bring local college OCF groups into a national campus ministry. The work of the Campus Commission proved to be especially important. During the decade of its effective existence, from 1965 to 1975, it gave a new generation of Orthodox Christians firsthand experience of Orthodox cooperation across jurisdictional and ethnic lines.

SCOBA began as a voluntary, advice-giving body. It had no authority to make decisions that would bind its member jurisdictions or to represent American Orthodoxy in an official way. But from the start, many of SCOBA's organizers hoped that it would become something more—that it would form the basis for a structurally united Orthodox church in America. From 1965 to 1968 SCOBA members discussed a series of proposals that would have transformed Orthodoxy in America from a collection of separate jurisdictions, each dependent on an Old World mother church, into a single independent church. These proposals called for official recognition of SCOBA as a provisional "Holy Synod of the Orthodox Church in America." Initially, at least, it would be headed by the exarch, or official representative, of the patriarch of Constantinople. Although each jurisdiction would continue to administer its own internal affairs, this new "Holy Synod" would be responsible for such matters as the ordination of bishops, common projects in areas such as education, and relations with other Orthodox churches around the world.

The problem, of course, was getting the mother churches in Europe and the Middle East to approve such proposals. At first some of the mother churches were favorably inclined, while others were strongly opposed. Despite this lack of agreement, the supporters of unity still had some grounds for optimism. For the first time in many decades, the Old World churches themselves were beginning to meet together to discuss issues of common concern. During the 1960s, a series of conferences brought together representatives of all the autocephalous churches to lay the groundwork for a future "Great and Holy Council of the Orthodox Church," which—if it ever met—would be the first gathering of its sort in modern times. Would it not be possible for these conferences to resolve the question of Orthodox unity in America? Unfortunately, the Old World churches continued to disagree on many issues. Tensions—particularly between the Patriarchate of Constantinople and the Russian Orthodox church—meant that the conferences would deal only with "safe" topics rather than with controversial issues such as the future of Orthodoxy in America. SCOBA's appeals to have its proposals taken up by a conference met with no success.

In the background lay an old problem: the relationship between the Metropolia and the Moscow patriarchate. The postwar revival of the Russian Orthodox church in the Soviet Union made it hard for other churches to continue to question its legitimacy. In the 1960s, assisted by the other Orthodox churches of Soviet-dominated Eastern Europe, the Moscow patriarchate was playing an increasingly active role in Orthodox affairs, such as cooperating with Constantinople in the project for a Great and Holy Council. At the same time, the Russian Orthodox church began to pressure Constantinople and the other autocephalous churches to end all relations with the Metropolia and other groups in the West that it regarded as schismatic. Representatives of the Moscow patriarchate within SCOBA regularly insisted that greater unity was not possible until all the participating jurisdictions were in good standing with their mother churches—and the Metropolia clearly was not in good standing with the Russian Orthodox church!

For its part, the Metropolia, unlike the Russian Orthodox Church Outside Russia, was willing to recognize the revived Moscow patriarchate as legitimate and to establish normal relations with it. After all, the independent path that the Metropolia had followed since 1924 was

Orthodox Unity in America

Many people hoped that the Standing Conference of Canonical Orthodox Bishops in America (SCOBA) would form the basis for a structurally united Orthodox church in America. This 1965 report of SCOBA's "Ad Hoc Commission on Unity" shows both the need for greater unity and the practical steps by which it might be achieved.

1. The necessity for greater unity. The urgent need for greater unity is self evident: Dogmatically—the Orthodox Church cannot claim to be the true, Holy, Catholic, and Apostolic Church if she is actually divided into a plurality of mutually independent, competing, and overlapping "jurisdictions." This division has long ago ceased to be justified by the peculiarities of Orthodox immigration in America and has become an open scandal to the faithful, a source of demoralization and dissatisfaction for the laity, and an obstacle to any effort and progress. Sociologically—the Orthodox still represent less than 2% of the American population. Divided into a dozen jurisdictions they simply cannot survive the growing pressure of the American "melting pot." Missionary—last but not least, our jurisdictional and national divisions virtually exclude all missionary expansion of Orthodoxy. No "jurisdiction" by itself can meet the urgent needs for better education, Orthodox presence on university campuses, in the public communications media, in philanthropic work, etc.

2. Unity and diversity. It would be unhealthy and unrealistic, however, to think of the much needed unification as a simple elimination of all diversities rooted in the national pluralism, or of American Orthodoxy as the creation of a "neutral" or "abstract" American Church. On the contrary, a living link and continuity with all that in the past constituted the treasure of Orthodoxy must not only be preserved but made a common heritage—the root of a fuller church

life here. The unity of the Orthodox in America must therefore be a unity in diversity in which both the demands of Orthodox ecclesiology and those of the living ecclesiological "memory" must be organically blended and maintained.

3. Unity by degrees. There can be no doubt that ultimately there shall exist in America one Orthodox Church unified in its canonical structure. But it would be absolutely impossible to simply "jump" into that ideal future. The unification of Orthodoxy must of necessity be achieved by degrees. The first degree is the canonical unification of the episcopate, since the unity of the episcopate is the organ of the Church's unity. Here a providential framework exists already—it is the Standing Conference. The next step would be its transformation into the canonical centre of American Orthodoxy. This can be achieved in the following way:

   (a) At its regular session the Standing Conference applies through its President to all autocephalous churches petitioning to be officially and canonically recognized as "The Holy Synod of the Orthodox Church in America." . . .

   (b) Prior to the canonical unification of all jurisdictions, and the elaboration of the permanent canonical structure of the American Church, the Exarch of the Ecumenical Patriarch will serve as ex officio the president of the Synod. Each national jurisdiction will be represented in the Synod by its head (one bishop per jurisdiction). . . .

   (c) Under the central canonical authority of the Holy Synod, and in all matters not specifically mentioned in its constitution, each jurisdiction will keep its actual autonomy and the present mode of self-government.

   (d) All questions involving two or more jurisdictions . . . will be solved by the Holy Synod.

   (e) The financial obligations of each national jurisdiction to her Mother Church will be decided by that jurisdiction itself.

originally intended to be temporary. But many members of the Metropolia feared that if they acknowledged the authority of the Moscow patriarchate they would lose their freedom to speak out against continuing religious oppression in the Soviet Union. More important, many in the Metropolia no longer regarded themselves as part of a "Russian" jurisdiction. By this point, the Metropolia had experienced many years of effective independence, during which its earlier Russian character had not been reinforced by the arrival of new immigrants. Instead, the church had assumed an increasingly American character. By the mid-1960s around 15 percent of its members were American converts to Orthodoxy, and the majority of its "cradle Orthodox" members spoke only English. At the Metropolia's 1967 "All-American Council," an overwhelming majority of clergy and members voted to change the church's official name from the unwieldy "Russian Orthodox Greek Catholic Church in America" to the simpler "Orthodox Church in America." The Metropolia's bishops considered the proposal premature; the church's official name would not be changed until 1970. But the vote does show that the Metropolia had come to identify itself as an American church.

The Metropolia faced a dilemma. It wanted to maintain its independence and distinctive character, but as the Moscow patriarchate increased its pressure on the other churches, it risked being isolated from the rest of the Orthodox world. In 1966 the Metropolia attempted to get around this dilemma. The Patriarchate of Constantinople claimed authority over the "diaspora," the Orthodox Christians living outside the limits of the other autocephalous churches. In the past the Patriarchate of Constantinople had accepted groups of Orthodox into its jurisdiction. Could it take in the Metropolia in the same way? The answer was no. During this period the Constantinople patriarchate was under considerable pressure from Moscow, and it refused the Metropolia's request. "You are Russians," the aged Patriarch Athenagoras told the Metropolia's representative. "Go back to your mother church. No one can solve your problem except the Russian Church."

In 1968 the Metropolia entered into a long series of discussions with the Russian Orthodox church in a new attempt to resolve the differences between them. In line with the policy of peaceful coexistence that then prevailed in Soviet-American relations, the Russian church softened its previous position. In 1970 the North American "daughter church" was reconciled to its Russian "mother church," and in turn the Russian church granted the Metropolia autocephaly, or full ecclesiastical independence, as the Orthodox Church in America (OCA). From the perspective of the Russian Orthodox church, the OCA was now a full member, albeit a junior member, in the family of Orthodox autocephalous churches—and also a likely ally in inter-Orthodox church politics.

Autocephaly resolved the old problem of the Metropolia's relationship to the Russian Orthodox church, but it created a new problem. Constantinople, together with the other Greek-led churches (Alexandria, Jerusalem, Cyprus, and Greece), refused to recognize the Metropolia's new status and name. They argued that only a pan-Orthodox council of ecumenical standing or the patriarch of Constantinople, acting as "first among equals," could establish a new autocephalous church. Moscow's unilateral actions in America therefore were illegitimate. On the other hand, a number of Orthodox churches in Eastern Europe (Bulgaria, Poland, Czechoslovakia, and Georgia) did recognize the autocephaly of the OCA. Still other churches (Antioch, Romania, and Serbia) adopted a wait-and-see attitude.

The Russian proclamation of the OCA's autocephaly touched off a storm of controversy in the Orthodox world that still has not completely subsided. On the international level, the issue of autocephaly, together with the closely related issues of the "diaspora" and autonomy, were added to the agenda of the future Great and Holy Council. Thus far, however, only limited progress has been made in discussion of the issue of autocephaly. Friendly discussions between the OCA and the Patriarchate of Constantinople have resumed in recent years, but continuing tensions between Constantinople and Moscow make full resolution of the status of the OCA unlikely in the near future.

In America, meanwhile, many had hoped that the independence of the OCA would advance the cause of Orthodox unity. Already in 1960, the Romanian Orthodox Episcopate of America had joined the

Children at this Romanian orphanage gather around a volunteer distributing goods. The Help for Romania Fund, established in 1989 by the Romanian Orthodox Episcopate of the Orthodox Church in America, is dedicated to improving the conditions of Romanian orphanages by sending food, medicines, bedding, and supplies.

Metropolia. Soon after the OCA became autocephalous, the Albanian Orthodox Archdiocese in America and the Bulgarian Orthodox Diocese also joined. The OCA had begun to recreate the multiethnic character of the Russian church's North American missionary archdiocese in the days before the Communist revolution had split the archdiocese into rival groups. In another noteworthy development, the OCA in 1977 elected Bishop Theodosius Lazor as its metropolitan, making him the first American-born head of any Orthodox jurisdiction in America. This reaffirmed the OCA's identification as an *American* Orthodox institution. But the autocephaly of the OCA did not spark wider unity among the Orthodox jurisdictions in America. In fact, practical cooperation between the jurisdictions declined. The OCA in the 1970s and 1980s proved no more able than SCOBA had been in the 1960s to bring about the full unity of Orthodox Christians in America.

Political developments in Europe in the 1990s had important consequences for relations among Orthodox churches in America and around the world. The collapse of communism in Russia and Eastern Europe gave the Orthodox churches there new freedom and opportunity for growth. In Russia, for example, the number of functioning parishes increased from around 8,000 in 1990 to 17,000 in 1997, and the number of dioceses increased from 67 to 123. The collapse of communism also meant that the Orthodox churches were now free to meet and work together with minimal interference from external political forces. Unfortunately, the collapse of communism also brought new tensions. For example, in 1996 the Russian Orthodox church and the Patriarchate of Constantinople came close to breaking off relations during a dispute over the status of the Orthodox churches in the newly independent republic of Estonia.

These developments in some ways brought Orthodox Christians in America closer together. Political issues that had divided many ethnic groups during the cold war period began to lose importance. Negotiations for reconciliation began. The new ethnic tensions and jurisdictional disputes of Europe did not carry over to America. If anything, they alerted Orthodox Christians in America to the dangers of extreme nationalism in religious matters and reminded them of how American they had become, regardless of their ethnic background or the church jurisdiction to which they belonged. Although the system of separate, parallel jurisdictions remained firmly entrenched, politics and ethnicity were losing their power to divide Orthodox Christians in America.

Meanwhile, other developments were changing the face of Orthodoxy in America. Since 1924 restrictive immigration laws had kept the number of new Orthodox arrivals in the United States very low. This changed with the Immigration Act of 1965, which opened the way for a new wave of immigration. Included among the "newest immigrants" were many Orthodox Christians. By 1980, Greek immigration was approaching its pre-1924 level. In the 1980s many Arab Orthodox Christians arrived in the wake of the civil war in Lebanon. In the 1990s, following the fall of communism in Russia and Eastern Europe, thousands of Russians, Ukrainians, Romanians, and Bulgarians began to arrive. Unlike the "new immigrants" at the turn of the century, these "newest immigrants" tended to be well-educated city-dwellers who quickly adjusted to American life. They also were less inclined than earlier immigrants to regard the Orthodox faith as an indispensable aspect of their lives. For a variety of reasons, the "newest immigrants" did not always fit in well in the parishes of the children, grandchildren, and great-grandchildren of the "new immigrants." The descendants of the "new immigrants" generally were very proud of their Old World heritage, but the "newest immigrants" tended to make fun of them, laughing at their attempts to speak their Old World language and at their outdated understanding of Old World culture. For their part, the descendants of the "new immigrants" often complained about how easy life was for the "newest immigrants" compared to what their parents—or grandparents or great-grandparents—had experienced when they came to America. All jurisdictions faced the challenge of ministering to these latest arrivals in America.

The "newest immigrants" have not been the only newcomers to Orthodox parishes in America. In the 1960s a steady stream of men and women from other religious backgrounds began to enter the Orthodox church. Since the 1970s that stream has become a flood. The active involvement of "converts" in church life has affected all the Orthodox jurisdictions, but it has been especially strong in the Antiochian Orthodox Christian Archdiocese and in the Orthodox Church in America, where nearly half of the priests now being ordained entered the Orthodox church as adults.

These converts to Orthodoxy are highly diverse. They do not conform to neat stereotypes. Some come from Christian denominations

A roadside billboard advertises Orthodox Christmas services. Here, as in other efforts to reach potential new church members, the Orthodox churches have demonstrated their adaptation to American ways.

with a strong liturgical tradition, which emphasizes the importance of worship and ritual, while others come from denominations and movements without such a tradition. Many have not been closely affiliated with any religious tradition at all. Some, particularly those who grew dissatisfied with recent trends in other Christian denominations, would describe themselves as having been "highly religious" before entering the Orthodox church, while others would describe themselves as having been "nonreligious." Some learned about Orthodoxy mainly through reading, others through personal contact. Most have entered the Orthodox church as individuals, after a long personal pilgrimage, while others entered as part of a larger group. One of the most striking journeys to Orthodoxy was that of a group of Evangelical Protestants who originally were engaged in youth ministry as part of the Campus Crusade for Christ in the 1960s. In 1977, after studying the Bible and extensive reading in early Christian texts, they formed an "Evangelical Orthodox Church." In 1987, after gaining a deeper acquaintance with the historic Orthodox church, they were received into the Antiochian Orthodox Christian Archdiocese as a group—approximately 2,000 people in 12 communities.

The presence of these converts has made Orthodoxy in America more diverse than ever—and less cohesive. Some converts are self-consciously American and eager to bring the message of Orthodoxy to mainstream America. They sometimes become impatient with "ethnics" who tend to take their Orthodox faith for granted or regard it as something appropriate only for "easterners." Some converts, impressed above all by the sense of stability and permanence they perceive in Orthodoxy, want to be as conservative and as traditional as possible, which has led to the introduction of "traditions" that most Orthodox Christians in America find rather unusual. For example, in parishes where such converts are numerous, women may be encouraged to wear head scarves in church. The entrance of many converts into the Orthodox church therefore has had an exhilarating but also an unsettling effect on parish life. The challenge of integrating these new members, like the challenge of ministering to the "newest immigrants," spans jurisdictional boundaries.

Another new situation facing all the Eastern Orthodox jurisdictions

The Orthodox contingent marches under its own banner in a March for Life in Washington, D.C. While still administratively divided, Orthodox Christians in America have begun to unite in issue-oriented action groups such as Orthodox Christians for Life.

has arisen from the growing presence of Oriental, or non-Chalcedonian, Orthodox Christians in America. In the early 20th century, Syrian Orthodox and Armenian Orthodox Christians were part of the "new immigration." Like the Eastern Orthodox ethnic groups, they organized their own dioceses in America, and later the Armenians suffered the political divisions that many Eastern Orthodox groups experienced as a result of Communist governments in their native lands. Since the mid-1960s, however, the number of Oriental Orthodox Christians in America has increased dramatically. Among the newcomers are thousands of Coptic (Egyptian), Indian, and Ethiopian Orthodox Christians—groups that were not earlier represented in the United States.

Their presence has revived discussion of issues that go back to the early days of Christianity. Since the 5th century, differences in belief have separated the Eastern Orthodox and Oriental Orthodox families of churches, but recent dialogue between high-level church leaders has concluded that these differences are more about wording than substance and that they need not continue to divide the churches. So far, however, the churches have not formally altered their old pronouncements against one another, and complete unity has not been officially restored. So how should these churches relate to each other in America, where their faithful often live and work together? Should the Eastern Orthodox help the Oriental Orthodox organize their own churches? In places where the Oriental Orthodox have no parishes, should they be encouraged to participate in the sacraments and other aspects of the life of the Eastern Orthodox parishes? People have answered these questions in many ways. Most leaders and faithful on both sides have encouraged closer relations between the two church families, but dissenting voices can also be heard on both sides. Not everyone is convinced that the other side is fully Orthodox.

If a few Eastern Orthodox Christians have questioned efforts to form closer ties with the Oriental Orthodox, many more have questioned Orthodox involvement in the modern ecumenical movement, which seeks to promote unity and cooperation among *all* Christian faiths. The Orthodox churches have been involved in this movement for wider Christian unity since its beginnings in the early 20th century. They have been members of the World Council of Churches (WCC) since its foundation in 1948, and in the United States the larger Orthodox jurisdictions have been members of the National Council of Churches of Christ (NCCC). But some Orthodox have criticized this involvement. One complaint is that such ecumenical bodies are dominated by liberal Protestant denominations whose concerns and favorite projects are increasingly at odds with Orthodox values. (The Orthodox churches tend to hold very conservative positions on abortion, homosexuality, and other ethical issues.) Others fear that Orthodoxy's claim to be the true church is weakened by association with non-Orthodox groups. The sharpest criticism has come from the Russian Orthodox Church Outside Russia and associated Old Calendarist Greek groups, which have described ecumenism as "a path which leads to the embrace of godless communism and prepares for the kingdom of the anti-Christ" and "a heresy against the dogma of the Church." Criticism is far less severe with-

The Greek Orthodox Archdiocese of America logo dramatically captures the scope of the jurisdiction's authority.

in the mainstream Orthodox jurisdictions, but more and more people, particularly Orthodox monks, are calling for reassessment of ecumenical involvement. Like many other issues in contemporary American Orthodoxy, the issue of ecumenism crosses jurisdictional lines. Even as ethnic differences and political issues lose their old power to divide, new issues like ecumenism are emerging that may in time prove equally divisive. As Orthodoxy in America becomes increasingly diverse, it also risks becoming increasingly fragmented.

The 1990s have brought some signs of a revival of the spirit of unity and cooperation that characterized the 1960s. For example, new inter-Orthodox agencies provide an opportunity for different jurisdictions to express their faith together in action. Particularly noteworthy has been the work of International Orthodox Christian Charities (IOCC), which representatives of the major Orthodox jurisdictions in America formed in 1992 to provide humanitarian aid in regions of the world affected by war and other disasters. Fully professional in its operations, the IOCC now has field offices in Moscow, Russia; Tbilisi, Georgia; Belgrade, Yugoslavia; Banja-Luka, Bosnia and Herzegovina; and Jerusalem, Israel. Another hopeful sign came in 1994, when 29 bishops from the member jurisdictions of SCOBA met at Antiochian Village, near Ligonier, Pennsylvania, in the largest gathering of its kind ever to take place in the United States. In the joint statements issued on this historic occasion, the bishops forcefully restated the need for a greater sense of mission and reaffirmed their commitment to the goal of visible Orthodox unity in America. Another impressive testimony to a renewed spirit of unity among Orthodox Christians in America came when a number of Old World patriarchs visited the United States during the 1990s. Although these leaders came primarily to visit members of their own spiritual flocks, they were enthusiastically welcomed by Orthodox Christians from across jurisdictional lines.

Despite these hopeful signs, it is unlikely that the Orthodox churches in America will be formally reorganized into a unified structure any time in the near future. The 1994 meeting of bishops at Ligonier rekindled American hopes for unity but aroused little or no enthusiasm among Orthodox church leaders abroad. The Patriarchate of Constantinople, for example, denounced the meeting as presumptuous and irregular. And although the visits of the Old World patriarchs generated considerable enthusiasm among all Orthodox Americans, their presence was a vivid reminder of American Orthodoxy's roots in Europe and the Middle East—and of the structural ties that link the faithful in America to the older churches.

Orthodox Christians in America are heirs to a tradition of outreach that goes back to the earliest centuries of Christianity. Their churches across America, from the oldest outposts in Alaska to the newest missions in the Sun Belt, are evidence of their eagerness to share their ancient faith with others. At the same time, they are linked to the Orthodox churches of the Old World by powerful emotional and structural ties. How can Orthodoxy become truly at home in America and reach out to Americans without sacrificing much of its rich cultural and spiritual heritage? This is the challenge facing Orthodox Christians in America today.

The Orthodox Churches at a Glance

THE EASTERN ORTHODOX CHURCHES

Listed in order of official rank, with estimates of membership, the autocephalous Eastern Orthodox churches are as follows:

- **The Patriarchate of Constantinople** (3,500,000 worldwide, chiefly in the large Greek Orthodox diaspora, or "dispersion," in Australia, Western Europe, and North America). Its head is often referred to as the ecumenical, or universal, patriarch and as "first among equals" of the bishops of the Orthodox world. The North American jurisdictions dependent on Constantinople include
    — The Greek Orthodox Archdiocese of America (2,000,000)
    — The Ukrainian Orthodox Church of the U.S.A. (100,000)
    — The Ukrainian Orthodox Church of Canada (129,000)
    — The American Carpatho-Russian Orthodox Greek Catholic Church (20,000)
    — The Albanian Orthodox Diocese of America (1,100)
    — The Belarusian Council of Orthodox Churches in North America (1,000)

- **The Patriarchate of Alexandria** (250,000, now chiefly in sub-Saharan Africa).

- **The Patriarchate of Antioch** (1,050,000 worldwide, chiefly in Syria and Lebanon but with a large diaspora in Australia and the Americas). Dependent on Antioch in North America is
    — The Antiochian Orthodox Christian Archdiocese (250,000)

- **The Patriarchate of Jerusalem** (260,000 in Israel and Jordan).

- **The Patriarchate of Moscow and All Russia** (120,000,000, chiefly in Russia, Ukraine, Belarus, and the Baltic states). Dependent on the Russian Orthodox church in the United States are
  — Parishes of the Russian Orthodox Church—Moscow Patriarchate (9,780)
- **The Patriarchate of Serbia** (8,000,000, chiefly in the former Yugoslavia but with a significant diaspora in Western Europe, Australia, and North America). Dependent on the Serbian Orthodox church in North America is
  — The Serbian Eastern Orthodox Church for the U.S.A. and Canada (140,000)
- **The Patriarchate of Romania** (19,000,000 chiefly in Romania, with a diaspora in Western Europe and North America). Dependent on the Romanian Orthodox church in North America is
  — The Romanian Orthodox Archdiocese in America and Canada (12,835)
- **The Patriarchate of Bulgaria** (8,000,000, chiefly in Bulgaria, with a small diaspora in Western Europe and North America). Dependent on the Bulgarian Orthodox church in North America is
  — The Bulgarian Eastern Orthodox Diocese (10,000)
- **The Georgian Orthodox church** (3,000,000)
- **The Church of Cyprus** (442,000)
- **The Church of Greece** (9,025,000)
- **The Orthodox Church of Poland** (570,000)
- **The Albanian Orthodox church** (160,000)
- **The Orthodox church in the Czech and Slovak Republics** (55,000) functions as an autocephalous church, and some other Orthodox churches regard it as such, but the Patriarchate of Constantinople and several other churches regard it as autonomous.
- **The Orthodox Church in America** (950,000), formerly the Russian Orthodox Greek Catholic Church of America, or the "Metropolia," functions as autocephalous and is recognized as such by some of the other Orthodox churches, but the Patriarchate of Constantinople and several other churches regard its status as irregular. Included in its membership are
  — The Romanian Orthodox Episcopate of America (65,000)
  — The Bulgarian Orthodox Diocese (10,000)
  — The Albanian Orthodox Archdiocese in America (30,000)

The autonomous Eastern Orthodox churches are

- **The Orthodox Church of Finland** (57,000)
- **The Orthodox Church of Japan** (30,000)

In addition to these autocephalous and autonomous churches, there are several other Orthodox groups whose status is irregular and which are not recognized by any of the other Orthodox churches. Two have significant followings in America: the Russian Orthodox Church Outside Russia (100,000), and various Old Calendarist Greek Orthodox churches (15,000).

THE ORIENTAL ORTHODOX CHURCHES

- **The Armenian Apostolic Church** (6,000,000 in Armenia and a large diaspora). In North America it includes two groups:
  — The Armenian Church of America (450,000)
  — The Prelacy of the Armenian Apostolic Church of America (350,000)
- **The Coptic Orthodox church** (3,900,000, chiefly in Egypt but with a growing diaspora in Western Europe, Africa, Australia, and the Americas). Dependent on it in North America is
  — The Coptic Orthodox Diocese (165,000)
- **The Ethiopian Orthodox church** (16,000,000). In the Americas it includes
  — The Ethiopian Orthodox Archdiocese (90,000)
- **The Syrian Orthodox church** (250,000 in Syria, Lebanon, and a small diaspora, and 1,000,000 in India). Dependent on it in North America is
  — The Syrian Orthodox Church of Antioch—Archdiocese of the United States and Canada (50,000)
- **The Malankara Orthodox Syrian church** (1,000,000 in India and a small diaspora). Dependent on it in the United States is
  — The Diocese of the Malankara Orthodox Syrian Church (50,000)
- **The Eritrean Orthodox church** (1,700,000 in Eritrea).

Glossary

Archimandrite   The head of a monastic community, comparable to an abbot. By extension, the term is used for a high-ranking unmarried priest appointed to assist a bishop in his administrative responsibilities.

Autocephaly   Ecclesiastical independence, from the Greek words *autos* and *kephale*, literally meaning "self-headed." A church is called **autocephalous** if it has the authority to manage its own affairs and to select all its own bishops, including its primate, without having to get the approval of a higher church authority.

Autonomy   Ecclesiastical self-governance, from the Greek words *autos* and *nomos*, literally meaning "self-ruled." A church is called **autonomous** if it has the authority to manage its own affairs but its primate must be approved by a higher church authority.

Canon law   The body of church laws or rules (canons).

Creole   An Alaskan-born person of Russian descent. Because government policy prohibited Russians from settling permanently in Alaska unless they married a native person, a creole was generally someone of mixed race.

Diaspora   A Greek word meaning "dispersion." It refers to people living outside of their native land.

Diocese   An ecclesiastical district under the jurisdiction of a bishop.

Divine liturgy   The term that Orthodox Christians most often use for their most important act of worship, the Holy Eucharist. It corresponds to the Roman Catholic Mass and to the service of Holy Communion in the Protestant churches.

Ecumenical council   An assembly of bishops convoked to settle a significant disciplinary or doctrinal issue and recognized as having universal authority in the church.

Ecumenical movement   A 20th-century movement to promote cooperation and greater unity among Christian churches.

Filioque   Latin meaning "and from the Son." The unilateral insertion of this word into the Nicene Creed in the West in the early Middle Ages became one of the main causes for the division of the Eastern and Western churches.

Heresy   A false teaching or belief.

Icon   An image, usually painted, representing Christ, the Virgin Mary, or other saints. A prominent feature inside an Orthodox church is the **iconostasis,** a screen adorned with icons that separates the altar area from the main body of the church building.

Jurisdiction   The authority of a bishop or other competent agent of church administration to govern in a particular situation. By extension, in America the term has come to apply to the church administration itself.

Monophysite   From the Greek words *monos* and *physis,* meaning "one nature." This term sometimes has been used for those churches that refused to accept the terminology of the Council of Chalcedon, A.D. 451, according to which Christ is "one person in two natures." Today the designation **Oriental Orthodox,** or sometimes non-Chalcedonian Orthodox, is preferred.

Primate   The chief or head bishop of a given region, from the Latin word *primus,* meaning "first." In the early church, the chief bishop of a province was usually called a **metropolitan,** because he was the bishop of the metropolis, or capital city, of the province. The chief bishop of a larger region was often called an **archbishop** or a **patriarch,** because he was the chief "father" of the people of the region. In modern Orthodox usage, the heads of the older or larger autocephalous churches usually have the title of patriarch, while those of the newer or smaller autocephalous or autonomous churches usually have the title of archbishop or metropolitan.

Schism   An illegitimate split or division in the church.

Uniate   Groups of Eastern Christians who entered into union, or **unia,** with the Roman Catholic Church, accepting its teachings while at the same time maintaining their Eastern forms of worship and other practices.

Chronology

325

First ecumenical council at Nicæa formulates creed

451

Council of Chalcedon leads to separation of the Oriental Orthodox churches

863

Mission of Sts. Cyril and Methodius to the Slavs

988

Conversion of Kievan Rus' (Ukraine, Russia) to Christianity

1054

Formal schism between Rome and Constantinople

1453

Fall of Constantinople to the Ottoman Turks

July 20, 1741

First Orthodox eucharistic liturgy in the New World

1768

Short-lived colony of Greeks in new Smyrna near St. Augustine, Florida

Sept. 24, 1794

Team of Russian Orthodox missionaries arrives on Kodiak Island, Alaska

1812

Russian-American Company establishes Fort Ross, in northern California

July 29, 1824

John (Innocent) Veniaminov arrives on Unalaska Island, Alaska

1828

Iakov Netsvetov ordained first native American Orthodox priest

Dec. 13, 1837

Death of St. Herman of Alaska

Dec. 15, 1840

Innocent Veniaminov ordained to be first Orthodox bishop in the New World

1864

First Greek Orthodox parish in the United States formed in New Orleans

Oct. 18, 1867

Russia sells Alaska to the United States

1870

Father Nicholas Bjerring organizes mission parish in New York City

March 25, 1891

St. Mary's parish in Minneapolis, led by Father Alexis Toth, enters the Orthodox church

1892

Greek Orthodox parishes formed in New York City and Chicago

1898

Bishop Tikhon Bellavin arrives in America

May 6, 1904

Raphael Hawaweeny becomes first Orthodox bishop ordained in America

Oct. 25, 1917

Communist revolution in Russia

Sept. 1921

Greek Orthodox Archdiocese of North and South America established by Archbishop (later Patriarch) Meletios Metaxakis.

1924

Russian North American Archdiocese (Metropolia) declares itself "temporarily self-governing"; National Origins Quota Act dramatically decreases Orthodox immigration

1930

Athenagoras Spirou named Greek Orthodox archbishop of America

1936

Metropolitan Antony Bashir heads Antiochian Orthodox Archdiocese

1944

Federated Orthodox Greek Catholic Primary Jurisdictions formed

1948

Archbishop Athenagoras elected patriarch of Constantinople

Oct. 26–27, 1956

Orthodox Christian Education Commission (OCEC) organized

1958

Archbishop Iakovos Coucouzes heads Greek Orthodox Archdiocese

March 15, 1960

Standing Conference of Canonical Orthodox Bishops in the Americas (SCOBA) organized

1961

First pan-Orthodox conference begins preparation for a still-awaited Great and Holy Council of the Orthodox Church

1965

Immigration Act allows new wave of Orthodox immigrants

April 10, 1970

Autocephaly of Orthodox Church in America (formerly Metropolia)

Aug. 9, 1970

Canonization of St. Herman of Alaska

1992

International Orthodox Christian Charities (IOCC) organized

Nov. 30– Dec. 1, 1994

Meeting of 29 Orthodox bishops from member jurisdictions of SCOBA at Ligonier, Pennsylvania

1996

Archbishop Spyridon Papageorgiou heads Greek Orthodox Archdiocese.

Further Reading

GENERAL

Ahlstrom, Sidney. *A Religious History of the American People.* New Haven: Yale University Press, 1972.

Butler, Jon, and Harry S. Stout, eds. *Religion in American History: A Reader.* New York: Oxford University Press, 1997.

Gaustad, Edwin. *A Religious History of America.* Rev. ed. San Francisco: Harper & Row, 1990.

Marty, Martin. *Pilgrims in Their Own Land: 500 Years of Religion in America.* New York: Penguin, 1985.

GENERAL WORKS ON ORTHODOXY

Litsas, Fotios K., ed. *A Companion to the Greek Orthodox Church.* New York: Greek Orthodox Archdiocese of North and South America, Department of Communication, 1984.

Meyendorff, John. *The Orthodox Church: Its Past and Its Role in the World Today.* 4th rev. ed. Crestwood, N.Y.: St. Vladimir's Seminary Press, 1996.

Ouspensky, Leonid, and Vladimir Lossky. *The Meaning of Icons.* Crestwood, N.Y.: St. Vladimir's Seminary Press, 1982.

Roberson, Ronald. *The Eastern Christian Churches: A Brief Survey.* 5th ed. Rome: Edizioni "Orientalia Christiana," 1995.

Schmemann, Alexander. *For the Life of the World: Sacraments and Orthodoxy.* Rev. ed. Crestwood, N.Y.: St. Vladimir's Seminary Press, 1982. This classic introduction to Orthodox liturgical spirituality was originally written for a conference of college students.

Ware, Timothy (Bishop Kallistos of Diokleia). *The Orthodox Church.* 2nd ed. Harmondsworth, Middlesex: Penguin, 1997.

———. *The Orthodox Way.* Rev. ed. Crestwood, N.Y.: St. Vladimir's Seminary Press, 1996.

GENERAL WORKS ON ORTHODOXY IN AMERICA

FitzGerald, Thomas E. *The Orthodox Church.* Denominations in America, no. 7. Westport, Conn.: Greenwood, 1995.

Garrett, Paul D. "Eastern Christianity." *Encyclopedia of the American Religious Experience.* Ed. Charles H. Lippy and Peter W. Williams. New York: Charles Scribner's Sons, 1988.

Pelikan, Jaroslav. "Orthodox Christianity in the World and in America." *World Religions in America: An Introduction.* Ed. Jacob Neusner. Louisville: John Knox Press, 1994.

[Surrency], Archimandrite Serafim. *The Quest for Orthodox Church Unity in America.* New York: Saints Boris and Gleb Press, 1973.

Tarasar, Constance J., and John H. Erickson, eds. *Orthodox America 1794–1976: Development of the Orthodox Church in America.* Syosset, N.Y.: Orthodox Church in America, Department of History and Archives, 1975.

Stokoe, Mark, with Leonid Kishkovsky. *Orthodox Christians in North America 1794–1994.* Syosset, N.Y.: Orthodox Christian Publications Center, 1995.

SPECIALIZED TOPICS

Afonsky, Gregory. *A History of the Orthodox Church in Alaska (1794–1917).* Kodiak, Alaska: Saint Herman's Theological Seminary, 1977.

Bobango, Gerald J. *The Romanian Orthodox Episcopate of America.* Jackson, Mich.: Romanian-American Heritage Center, 1979.

Corey, George S., *et al.,* eds. *The First One Hundred Years: A Centennial Anthology Celebrating Antiochian Orthodoxy in America.* Englewood, N.J.: Antakya Press, 1995.

Efthimiou, Miltiades B., and George A. Christopoulos, eds. *History of the Greek Orthodox Church in America.* New York: Greek Orthodox Archdiocese of North and South America, 1984.

Garrett, Paul D. *St. Innocent, Apostle to America.* Crestwood, N.Y.: St. Vladimir's Seminary Press, 1979.

Garvey, John. "Religion: Eastern Orthodoxy." *The Atlantic Monthly.* May 1989, pp. 30–37.

Koulomzin, Sophie. *Many Worlds: A Russian Life.* Crestwood, N.Y.: St. Vladimir's Seminary Press, 1980.

Kuropas, Myron B. *The Ukrainian Americans: Roots and Aspirations 1884–1954.* Toronto: University of Toronto Press, 1991.

Magocsi, Paul Robert. *The Carpatho-Rusyn Americans.* New York: Chelsea House, 1989.

———. *The Russian Americans.* New York: Chelsea House, 1989.

Mathewes-Green, Frederica. *Facing East: A Pilgrim's Journey into the Mysteries of Orthodoxy.* San Francisco: HarperCollins, 1997.

Oleksa, Michael. *Orthodox Alaska: A Theology of Mission.* Crestwood, N.Y.: St. Vladimir's Seminary Press, 1992.

Oleksa, Michael, ed. *Alaskan Missionary Spirituality.* New York: Paulist Press, 1987.

Papaioannou, George. *From Mars Hill to Manhattan: The Greek Orthodox in America under Athenagoras I.* Minneapolis: Light and Life, 1976.

Saloutos, Theodore. *The Greeks in the United States.* Cambridge, Mass.: Harvard University Press, 1964.

———. "Growing Up in the Greek Community of Milwaukee," *Historical Messenger of the Milwaukee County Historical Society.* Vol. 29.2, pp. 46–60.

Sheler, Jeffery L. "Discovering Byzantium." *U.S. News and World Report.* October 20, 1997, pp. 60–63.

Smith, Barbara. *Orthodoxy and Native Americans: The Alaskan Mission.* Syosset, N.Y.: Orthodox Church in America, Department of History and Archives, 1980.

Index

Acknowledgments

Writing a book for young people is difficult for someone whose usual abode is the library. Friends and associates with special expertise have helped in many ways. These include the personnel of the Milwaukee County Historical Society; my good friend Mr. George Soldatow; my student Fr. Andrew Kostadis; my counterpart at Holy Cross Greek Orthodox School of Theology, Prof. Lewis Patsavos; the librarian of St. Vladimir's Orthodox Theological Seminary, Miss Eleana Silk; and especially the archivist of the Orthodox Church in America, Mr. Alexis Liberovsky, an unfailing source of information and assistance. Thanks also is due Jon Butler and Harry Stout, who invited me to undertake this project, and Nancy Toff and Casper Grathwohl for their invaluable editorial work. But most helpful of all have been my students at St. Vladimir's Seminary, on whom I test-marketed many of my ideas, and my sons Paul and David, who had the patience to read through successive drafts of my text. I dedicate this book to them.

Picture Credits

Alaska State Library: 33; Alaska State Museum, Juneau: 36; Anchorage Museum of History and Art: 10; Boston Public Library, Print Department: 6, 109, 110; Florida State Archives: 72; Greek Orthodox Archdiocese of America: 126; New York Public Library / St. Vladimir's Seminary Press: 20; Orthodox Church in America: 13, 26, 30, 32, 34, 38, 39, 41, 43, 44, 45, 47, 50, 52, 56, 64, 68, 74, 76, 81, 84, 93, 94, 97, 102, 107, 112, 114, 120, 122; Public Relations Department, Diocese of the Armenian Church of America: 2; St. Petersburg Times: 14; St. Tikhon's Orthodox Theological Seminary: 124; Gary Tong: 19; The University of Illinois at Chicago, The University Library, Jane Addams Memorial Collection, Wallace Kirkland Papers: 88, 90, 92; University of Notre Dame Archives: 67; Vanni/Art Resource: 24.

Text Credits

Page 40: "Instructions . . . to the Missionary of Nushagak, Theophanus, Hieromonk," reprinted in *American Orthodox Messenger,* vol. 3 no. 20 (1899), with English translation in vol. 3, no. 21.

Page 48: Priest-Monk Dionysius, "The Main Problems and the Character of Russian Orthodox Foreign Mission Work Compared to Western Non-Orthodox Mission Work," *American Orthodox Messenger,* vol. 5, no. 6 (1901).

Page 58: *Orthodox America, 1794–1976: Development of the Orthodox Church in America.* Constance Tarasar and John H. Erickson, eds. Syosset, N.Y.: Orthodox Church in America, Department of History and Archives, 1975.

Page 66: "The Archpriest John Naumovich As Viewed by the Uniate Viestnik," *American Orthodox Messenger,* vol. 2, no. 1 (1897), trans. George Soldatow, *Archpriest Alexis Toth: Letters, Articles, Papers and Sermons.* Vol. 4. Minneapolis: AAROM Press, 1988. Slightly modified.

Page 84: *Fifty-fifth Anniversary Booklet,* St. Nicholas Russian Orthodox Greek Catholic Church, Joliet, Illinois, 1962.

Page 106: Based on the author's oral history interviews with Mrs. Annette Milkovich, August–September, 1997.

Page 117: Archimandrite Seraphim (Surrency), *The Quest for Orthodox Church Unity in America.* New York: Saints Boris and Gleb Press, 1973.

John H. Erickson

John H. Erickson is Professor of Canon Law and Church History and Associate Dean for Academic Affairs at St. Vladimir's Orthodox Theological Seminary, Crestwood, N.Y. A former chairman of the Department of History and Archives of the Orthodox Church in America, he is the author of *The Challenge of Our Past: Studies in Orthodox Canon Law and Church History* and (with John Borelli) *The Quest for Unity: Orthodox and Catholics in Dialogue.*

Jon Butler

Jon Butler is the William Robertson Coe Professor of American Studies and History and Professor of Religious Studies at Yale University. He received his B.A. and Ph.D. in history from the University of Minnesota. He is the coauthor, with Harry S. Stout, of *Religion in American History: A Reader,* and the author of several other books in American religious history including *Awash in a Sea of Faith: Christianizing the American People,* which won the Beveridge Award for the best book in American history in 1990 from the American Historical Association.

Harry S. Stout

Harry S. Stout is the Jonathan Edwards Professor of American Christianity at Yale University. He is the general editor of the Religion in America series for Oxford University Press and co-editor of *Readings in American Religious History, New Directions in American Religious History, A Jonathan Edwards Reader,* and *The Dictionary of Christianity in America.* His book *The Divine Dramatist: George Whitefield and the Rise of Modern Evangelicalism* was nominated for a Pulitzer Prize in 1991.

MB
Rel
eastern orthodox